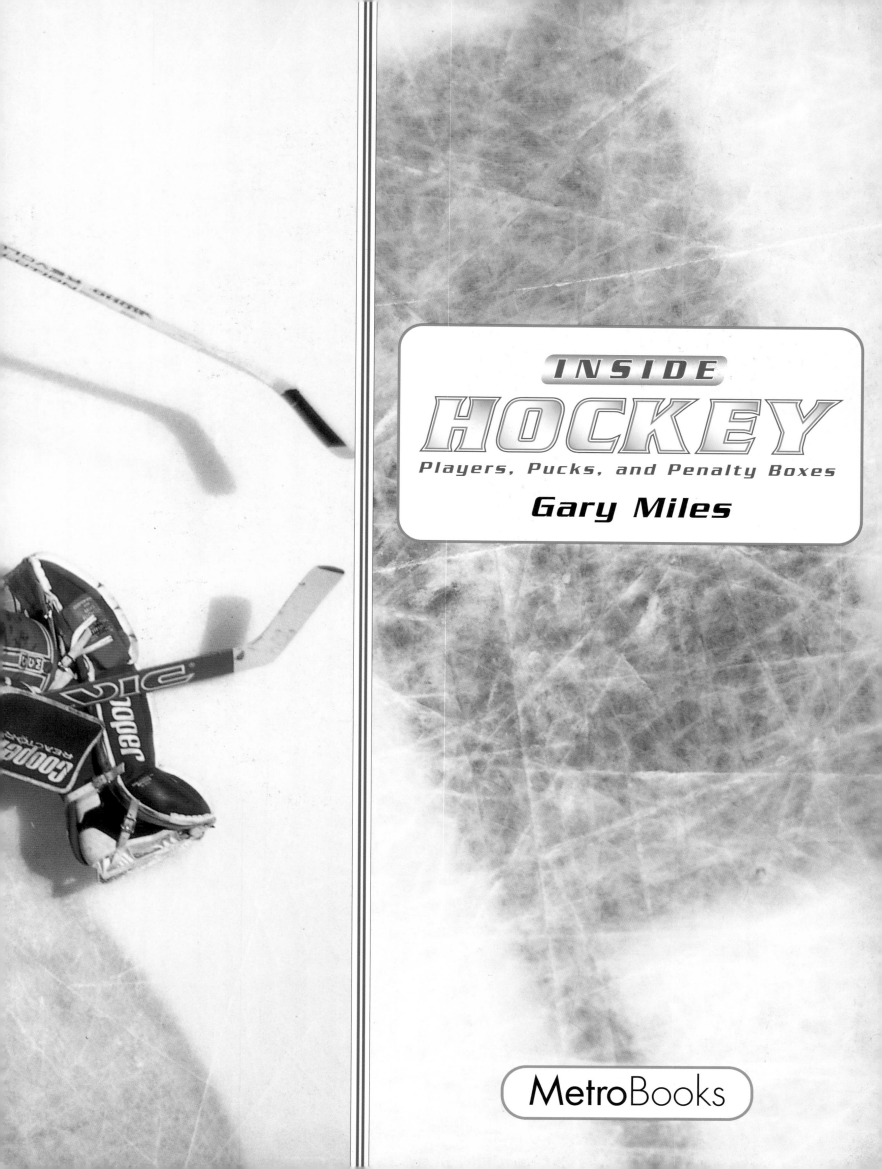

INSIDE
HOCKEY
Players, Pucks, and Penalty Boxes

Gary Miles

MetroBooks

An Imprint of Friedman/Fairfax Publishers

© 1998 by Michael Friedman Publishing Group, Inc.

Library of Congress Cataloging-in-Publication Data available upon request.

ISBN 1-56799-702-3

Editors: Ben Boyington and Stephen Slaybaugh
Art Director: Jeff Batzli
Designers: Garrett Schuh and Diego Vainesman
Photography Editor: Karen Barr
Production Manager: Jeanne Hutter

Color separations by HK Scanner Arts Int'l Ltd.
Printed in The United Kingdom by Butler and Tanner Limited

For bulk purchases and special sales, please contact:
Friedman/Fairfax Publishers
Attention: Sales Department
15 West 26th Street
New York, NY 10010
212/685-6610 FAX 212/685-1307

Visit our website:
http://www.metrobooks.com

DEDICATION

For Shelby. Thanks for being you.

ACKNOWLEDGMENTS

Many thanks to the hockey men and women who graciously gave their time, insights, and wisdom to this project: Brian Burke, Terry Murray, Bill Barber, Scotty Bowman, Kevin Haller, Bill Torrey, Eric Lindros, Ed Jovanovski, Ron Wilson, Jari Kurri, Wayne Gretzky, Craig MacTavish, Joe Watson, Gary Dornhoefer, Pat Conacher, Gerry Cheevers, Bob Clarke, Mike Bossy, Theoren Fleury, Mark Messier, Dale Hawerchuk, Mikael Renberg, John Vanbiesbrouck, Kevin Dineen, Shjon Podein, Ron Hextall, Larry Robinson, Kevin McDonald, Joe Kadlec, Shawn Antoski, Doug MacLean, Rod Brind'Amour, Jacques Demers, Terry Carkner, Bill Guerin, Zack Hill, Rob Parent, and the entire administrative staff of the NHL.

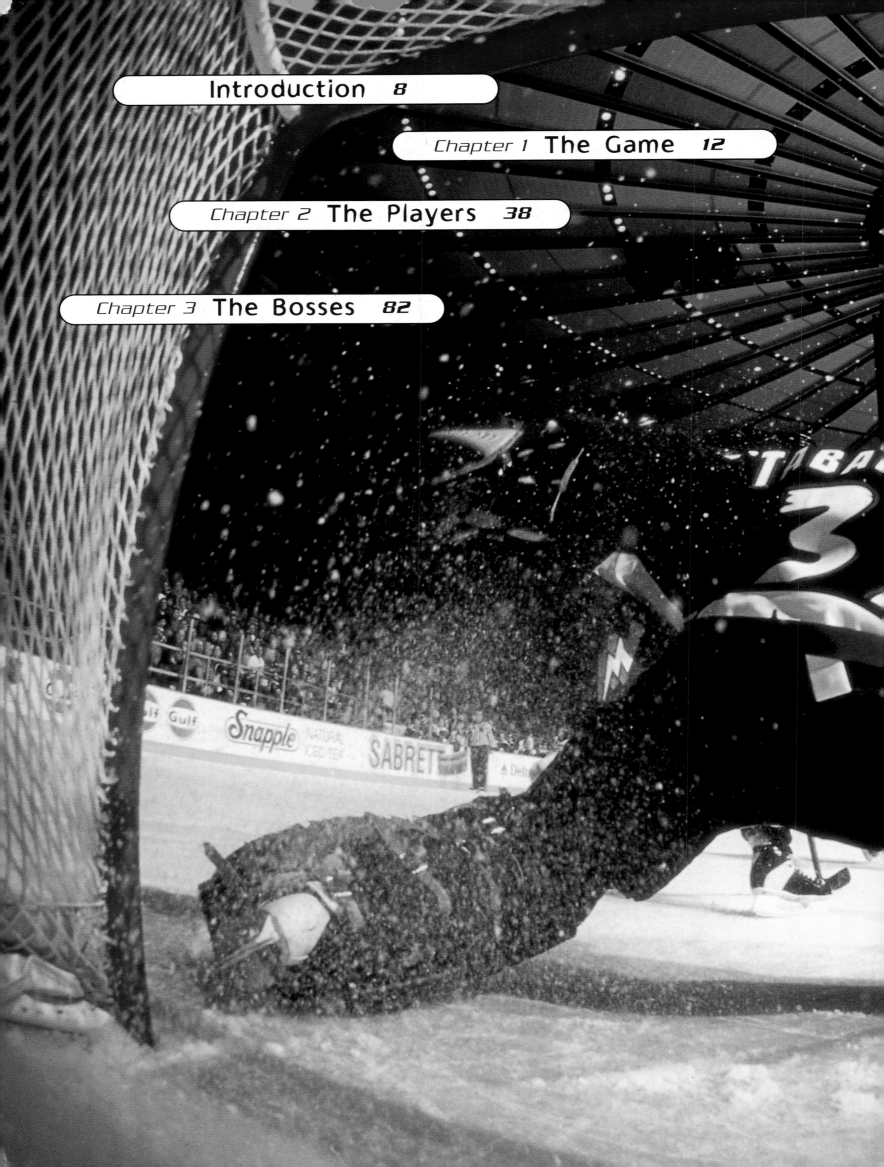

During the long, cold, empty winter of 1994–95, hockey fans in North America became keenly aware of the truth of the old adage that you never know how much you miss something until it's gone.

Most observers knew long before winter that hockey that season just wouldn't be the same. The players and team owners in the National Hockey League (NHL) failed to reach a collective-bargaining agreement by the time August rolled into September, and the world's premier hockey league not only missed the glitz and glamour of opening night but actually shut down for 101 days. The rinks were dark and fans scrambled for something else to do. For some people, especially those diehards in Canadian cities who revel in the game's rough-and-tumble ways, the loss was devastating. Sports bars nearly went bankrupt, and TV programmers hustled daily to fill the suddenly available hours of air time. Disgruntled fans filed lawsuits to get the games going again. Players blamed management for the labor problems, and management blamed the players. Tempers flared like wildfires during the contentious negotiations.

Hockey was still being played in the minor leagues and at colleges across North America. The European leagues flourished, especially those in Finland and Sweden. But the best players in North America were idle. "It's tough on people," said Cliff Fletcher, a long-time NHL executive with teams in St. Louis, Atlanta, Calgary, and Toronto. "Hockey is in the fabric of our society."

Indeed, for millions of people, hockey is much more than a game. It's not an exaggeration to say that, for some, hockey is a way of life. Millions of people have played professional and amateur hockey all over the world, and many millions of children spend years of their lives playing almost daily in homemade rinks of all kinds. That's why such passions were stirred when the NHL shut down for nearly half a season. Because the game is played

in backyard and local rinks by youngsters as soon as they can skate, it becomes part of their routines—their schedules are built around the game. And this passion for hockey does not end with the kids; adults have it too. If not for passion for the game (and maybe for the championship trophy), why would the Dawson City hockey club, a rugged squad of miners and adventurers based in the Yukon, have traveled 4,400 miles (7,040km) by dogsled, boat, and train, only to lose back-to-back games to Ottawa, 9–2, and 23–2, in the 1905 Stanley Cup finals?

Like those of hockey's big brothers—baseball, football, and basketball—hockey's history is so filled with tradition and drama that fans don't simply enjoy the game: they live through it. Hockey fans still shiver when they recall Bobby Orr's fabulous acrobatic goal that won the Cup for the Boston Bruins in 1970. They marvel at Mark Messier guaranteeing a victory for the New York Rangers before Game Six of the 1994 Eastern Conference finals against the New Jersey Devils—and then delivering 3 goals in the third period to make it happen. The Flyers' 35-game winning streak in 1979–80 is still remembered fondly in Philadelphia. And fans in Denver, who embraced a team that relocated there from Quebec in 1995, are still giddy about the fabulous triple-overtime victory of the Colorado Avalanche over the upstart Florida Panthers in Game Four of the 1996 Cup finals.

Hockey Night in Canada is a veritable television institution, with millions of Canadians tuning in regularly, and ESPN and the Fox network are embracing hockey in the United States. Every weekend, millions of people—families and friends—gather around the television and root for their favorite players and teams. Dinners are often scheduled around the games. Nearly every Canadian player can recall snowy evenings spent at home watching the Montreal Canadiens or the Toronto Maple Leafs on television. "It's part of your life," says Terry Murray, a native of Shawville, Quebec, who first played in the NHL and then went on to coach with the Washington Capitals and Philadelphia Flyers. "You grow up with it." For former players such as Bill Barber, who cut his hockey teeth in Kitchener with the Ontario Hockey League, hockey became a way of life early. In the 1960s, there were no video or computer games to occupy a young boy's time. "You had to go make your own fun," Barber says. "And our fun was playing hockey. You'd get a bunch of guys together on a pond, the puck was dropped, and you'd play there all day."

After Scott Mellanby killed a rat in the dressing room at Miami Arena, Florida Panthers fans adopted the rodent as their mascot during the 1996 playoffs. They showered the ice with plastic rats after every Panthers goal.

All this despite—or perhaps because of—the violence inherent to the sport. To be a hockey player, you have to be tough—very tough. Broken teeth, scars that run jaggedly up and down the face, and gnarled fingers are all ordinary parts of game. Face masks and helmets are relatively new. Hockey players and fans thrive on this danger, and they'll do whatever they can to play whenever they can. The pros, for instance, have aluminum sticks and skates that have inflatable pads to cushion their feet; their equipment is state-of-the-art. But for the twelve-year-old down the street, cardboard can serve as goalie pads; for the college kids in the parking lot, half of a tennis ball is as good as a puck; and for the little girl on the frozen pond north of Montreal, a tree branch stands in for a full-fledged stick.

"Hockey players are far different from other athletes," says Barber, an NHL Hall of Famer with the Flyers who went on to scout and then coach in the

American Hockey League (AHL). "Most of them came up in a different background where there weren't a lot of handouts. You have to really battle and work hard and get through the system. It's a tough sport. You play 80 games a season, and I never even played in an indoor rink or on artificial ice until I was fourteen years old."

Such sacrifices left Barber and other youngsters like him with frozen feet and chapped hands. But every day they'd go back to the pond and play. They never wore helmets. Their winter coats were their uniforms. "Your fingers would hurt because you used your own gloves from home," Barber says. "You cried when you were young. But it went on, and you'd go out there every day just because you loved the game."

Even the NHL's championship trophy is different from any other trophy. Do you know the names of the Super Bowl trophy, the World Series trophy, or the NBA championship trophy? Probably not. But you've certainly heard of the Stanley Cup. The oldest trophy in professional sports, the Stanley Cup draws huge crowds whenever it is displayed. During the playoff finals, men, women, and children of all ages stand in line for hours to view the Cup and the NHL's other trophies in the host cities. One of seventeen trophies awarded after each NHL season, the Cup is so valued these days that a security guard is hired to look after it 24 hours a day. Of course, the Cup that this guard protects is a replica; the original Stanley Cup sits in the Hockey Hall of Fame in Toronto.

Oleg Tverdovsky (left) is one of the NHL's rising young defensemen. With his passing and skating skills, he's been compared to New York Rangers star Brian Leetch.

For some Canadians, hockey was the best game in town because it was the only game in town. "We didn't have any baseball in Canada until maybe twenty years ago," says Scotty Bowman, the coach with the most wins in NHL history. "We had pro football, but people knew that NHL hockey was the best in the world. There wasn't a lot of infiltration of the other sports yet."

Hockey is a simple game: the offense tries to hit the puck into the net; the defense tries to stop them. But when you mingle near-impossible accomplishments, heartbreaking failures, and all the accompanying sensations of joy and grief in between with the mechanics of the game, it turns the experience into a swirling, intriguing, exciting game that will never die.

"I've enjoyed hockey my whole life," says Kevin Haller, who won a gold medal with Team Canada in the 1990 World Junior Championship and a Stanley Cup ring with the 1993 Montreal Canadiens. "So to be able to play a game that you enjoy so much for your job—it's quite fulfilling and exciting."

Origins

"Because the guys are on skates things happen so fast."

SHJON PODEIN,
Philadelphia Flyers

although Canada, the United States, Russia, and the Czech Republic all claim to be home to the best hockey players in the world today, historians who dig for the roots of the game usually wind up crediting Great Britain with hosting the first hockey games. Of course, the game in the very early days resembled today's game only in the fact that it was played on ice and the idea was to knock an object past the other team. There weren't any goalposts in the early days, only piles of snow to mark the goals. There were no stands for fans or benches for the players. There was only the rough-edged playing surface and the players, who used crude sticks and makeshift pucks.

It's obvious why hockey got its start in the cold, foggy marshlands of the British Isles: weather. When the frigid British winters set in, the shallow marshes would freeze and the people would take to the ice. Around 1820, a new sport started to catch on among the visitors to the frozen lakes. People had played field hockey and another game, known as "bandy," in Europe for years. But this new version of the old sport required that its players put on skates, which had been used and developed mostly in the Netherlands years before, and take to the ice. Using metal blades that could be strapped to their boots, the players would cut branches from trees to use as sticks; for pucks they would use round pieces of cork or wooden

Opposite: The rules may have changed over the years but the importance of hustle hasn't. Shjon Podein (25) shows how it's done by racing after a puck in front of the opposing goaltender.

Above: The speed and excitement of hockey made it popular long before players wore equipment and played for huge salaries.

balls. Like the rules at that time, the equipment and the rinks were far different from those of the modern game. In the early days, the goal measured 12 feet by 7 feet (3.7m × 2.1m) (as opposed to today's 6 feet by 4 feet [1.8m × 1.2m]). In the 1870s, each team was made up of nine players skating at the same time, and bodychecking was not permitted. There were no substitutions, so players were expected to play the entire 60 minutes of the game.

By 1880, the game had begun to grow into the game we know today: the teams were reduced to seven-man units. The puck replaced the ball, and sticks were flattened on both sides to allow players to handle the puck better. The equipment also improved. Pads and gloves that players used in cricket and baseball were used to protect the legs and hands of hockey players. Before this time, players had used anything they could get their hands on for protection, including department store catalogs, newspapers, cardboard, and books. (In an odd twist more than a hundred years later, on September 13, 1996, Charlie O'Brien, a catcher for baseball's Toronto Blue Jays, wore a mask designed like a modern goalie mask in a game against the New York Yankees.)

Although hockey was taking root in several European countries, it didn't start to become truly organized until it became popular in Canada. When the long, cold northern winters left the British soldiers stationed there with nothing to do, they filled their empty hours by playing hockey. Like that of baseball, which was developing and growing at about the same time, the exact origin of formal hockey is unknown. Some historians report that the first formal game was played in Kingston, Ontario, in 1867. The bored soldiers shoveled off frozen Kingston Harbor and played what came to be known as the unofficial first game of hockey.

After that, Kingston became a hockey hotbed. It claimed to be the home of the first hockey league in North America. Four teams—the Athletics, the Kingstons, Royal Military College, and Queens University—comprised the league in 1885, and the Athletics beat Queens University for the first championship. By this time, hockey had become very popular, and crowds had begun showing up at games. Thus, the ticket was born. Kingston may or may not have been the home of hockey, but other Canadian towns were playing the game on their ponds and at rinks. Games were reported to have been played in the 1870s by soldiers stationed in Halifax, Nova Scotia, and by students at McGill University in Montreal. The Montreal Gazette had a reference to a hockey game in its pages in 1875, and reporters later wrote about a new thing called a "puck."

Regardless of where the first formal game was played, it soon became obvious that Canada, with its long winters and frozen ponds and lakes, would become the hockey capital of the world. Rules were soon codified, and Arthur Farrell of Montreal's Shamrock Hockey Club was credited with writing down the first set of regulations. What a different game it was then! The rinks were smaller than they are today, but Farrell still felt it necessary to play seven men to a side, as compared to the five that skate together in today's larger rinks. Imagine how crowded the ice was in those games! With the game becoming more organized, the need for a championship trophy soon arose. So Sir Frederick Arthur Stanley, the sports-minded governor general of Canada, directed his assistant, Lord Kilcoursie, to spend $48.67 Canadian ($50 U.S.) on the creation of a silver bowl with a gold interior. Lord Stanley decreed that the bowl, first called the Dominion Hockey Challenge Cup but eventually renamed the Stanley Cup in his honor, would go to the best hockey team in the land. The Montreal Amateur Athletic Association won the first Stanley Cup in 1893 after going 7–1 in a playoff series against four other clubs.

As the game moved into the twentieth century, it grew by amazing leaps and bounds. Leagues were formed by colleges and factories, and some of the best players started earning salaries to play in leagues such as the Federal League, the Eastern Canada League, and the Eastern Canada Hockey Association. Fred "Cyclone" Taylor, one of the game's early stars, was paid $5,000 to play a single season. In 1910, to keep players fresh during a game, the National Hockey

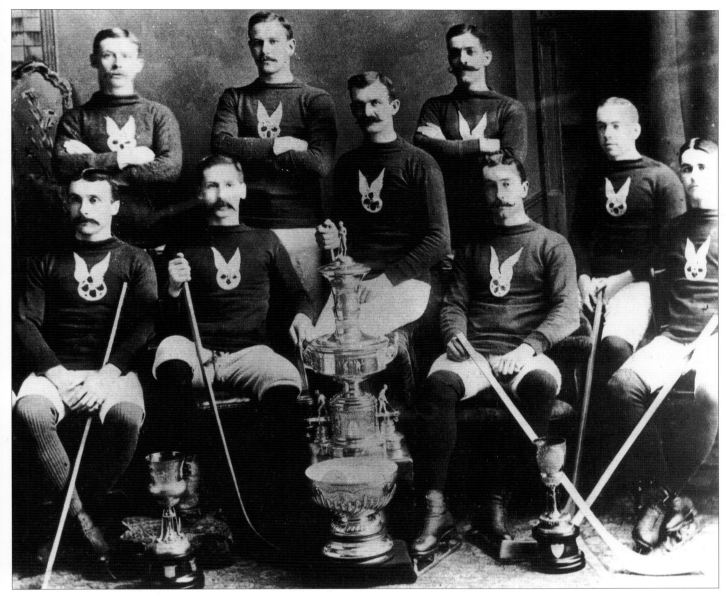

Association of Canada, the predecessor of the NHL, changed the structure of the game from two 30-minute periods to three 20-minute periods. The next season, they cut the number of players on the ice for one team from seven to six. In 1917, the rules were changed to allow goalies to drop to the ice to make a save. Before that, goalies had to remain upright while stopping the puck or they would be penalized.

As the years passed, the rules were changed to make the game faster and more exciting for its growing fan base. The first blue lines, which kept attacking players onside when the puck was carried from one end of the rink to the other, appeared in 1918, and goaltenders were permitted to pass the puck beginning in 1921. Forward passes, not allowed in the defending and neutral zones before 1927, became legal that year. Flooding the rink so the ice was fresh for the next period was made obligatory in 1940. The red line, designed to speed up the game and reduce offside calls, appeared in 1943. By most accounts, that rule signaled the beginning of the game's modern era—its golden era.

"The tension in a hockey game, with the quickness of the play—you don't see that in any other sport," says Shjon Podein of the Philadelphia Flyers. "You get so excited. Your ups and downs come just like that watching the game, and it's the same way playing it. In baseball and football, whistles are always stopping the play."

The Montreal Athletic Association won the first Stanley Cup in 1893. Champions of the Amateur Hockey Assocation that season, the team also won the Cup in 1894, 1902, and 1903.

Fred "Cyclone"
Taylor, the sport's
first high-paid star,
poses in his
Vancouver uniform.

Brian Burke, the NHL's senior vice president and director of hockey operations, says that hockey has taken the best aspects of all sports and incorporated them into the game. "If you like speed, hockey is the fastest game played without machines," says Burke. "If you like hitting, boy, do we have hitting. The goaltending is a uniquely exciting part of our game, and we have the world's greatest athletes. Everything that NBA players have to do—pass, shoot, play defense, score—our guys have to do...on steel blades that are an eighth of an inch wide. Just being able to skate at the NHL level is an amazing athletic feat. We also have the greatest athletes in terms of personality and character. Their willingness to play hurt. Their commitment to team success. It's the only game where a goal and an assist have the same value. Our guys, when they get stitched up, don't even get a painkiller. They'll play with injuries that would keep other athletes out for weeks."

The National Hockey League

"The hotels are all the same.
The travel gets to you,
but the new faces keep you fresh
and there is always something new,
something different going on."

ERIC LINDROS,
Philadelphia Flyers

the National Hockey League is a direct descendant of the National Hockey Association of Canada. When that old league fell apart, four clubs—the Montreal Canadiens, Montreal Wanderers, Ottawa Senators, and Quebec Bulldogs—banded together at a meeting in Montreal in 1917 to form the NHL. The Toronto Arenas were admitted to the league as a fifth team before the 1918 season began.

As is the case with most fledgling leagues, there were troubles at the start for NHL organizers. The Bulldogs couldn't quite pull everything together for that first 22-game season, so they dispersed their players to the other four teams. A year later, a fire ripped through the Montreal Arena, sending both the Canadiens and the Wanderers out into the street. The Wanderers folded, never to be heard from again, and the Canadiens were forced to play their games in tiny Jubilee Rink.

It's sometimes not easy to skate—forwards or backwards—with that crazy piece of frozen rubber. Defenseman Todd Gill (left) and center Ray Ferraro eye up a bouncing puck during a game between the Sharks and the Kings in 1996.

But as the years slipped by, the NHL gained stability and recognition. The 1922–23 season saw famed sportscaster Foster Hewitt broadcast the first NHL game on the radio. A spectacular 10,000-seat arena went up in Ottawa in 1923, and Boston was awarded the first U.S. franchise. In 1924 the Montreal Forum, perhaps the most famous hockey rink in the world, opened, and the league expanded to six teams and a 30-game schedule. In 1926 the New York Rangers and Chicago Blackhawks entered the league, the first indication of a swing south that would later cause Canadians to fear that their national sport was being purloined by the Americans. Indeed, only two of the league's six teams in 1942— Montreal and Toronto—were in Canada. The other four were in Boston, Chicago, Detroit, and New York.

By the end of the 1926–27 season, the NHL had expanded to ten teams and had come to feature both American and Canadian divisions. It was that season in which the Stanley Cup became the symbol of the NHL champion. Before then, the NHL champion had played the champion of one of two other developing leagues, the Western or Pacific Coast leagues, for the Cup. In the 1930–31 season, some of the teams organized farm teams, and the four-sided scoreboard was introduced at many arenas. Players began wearing numbers on their sweaters for easier identification. In 1931 Maple Leaf Gardens, perhaps the second-most-famous hockey rink, opened to the public. Despite all these advances, money was still tight in the league. St. Louis applied for a franchise in 1932 but was rejected because the northern clubs couldn't afford to travel there. In 1938, players were given $5 a day for food and $2.50 for accommodations.

Although the first All-Star Game—a benefit for an injured player, Ace
Bailey—was played in the 1933–34 season, the All-Star Game as we know it
today was first played in 1947 and benefitted the players' new pension fund.
Although the NHL remained a six-team league from 1942 to 1967, it enjoyed
years of tremendous growth and popularity. In 1954, the league announced that
its officials would wear black-and-white striped shirts. In 1961 the Hockey Hall
of Fame opened in Toronto. Then expansion struck. Six new teams—the
California Golden Seals, Los Angeles Kings, Minnesota North Stars,
Philadelphia, Pittsburgh Penguins, and the St. Louis Blues—joined the league in
1967. The Buffalo Sabres and Vancouver Canucks joined in 1970. Kansas City
Scouts and Washington Capitals entered in 1974. By 1975 the NHL had grown to
two nine-team conferences and an 80-game schedule. In 1979 four teams from the
defunct World Hockey Association—the Edmonton Oilers, Hartford Whalers,
Quebec Nordiques, and the Winnipeg Jets—joined the league.

In those days, there was a great deal of holding and grabbing, which slowed
down the game. Today, there are rules to eliminate much of this physical contact.
"You had to fight through checks to get to the net back then," says former Flyers
left winger Bill Barber. "I liked it like that because there were no givens. We
called it the War Zone. You went in there and fought your way through that.
Then, when you got there, look out, because you knew you were going to get
lumbered on. You had to pay a heavy price to score a goal."

The 1990s saw the NHL fall victim to labor problems between the clubs
and the players. The 1991–92 season was suspended for eleven days when the

players went on strike for a better collective-bargaining agreement. In 1994–95, a total of 468 games were canceled when the clubs locked out the players in another contract dispute. Although the labor disputes were eventually settled, the disruption of the game hurt the newer clubs, which were already scrounging for customers. "It hurt us a lot," says Bill Torrey, the president of the expansion Florida Panthers. "Our first year we had over nine thousand season-ticket holders. During the lockout, we lost about twelve hundred (to) thirteen hundred of them."

Of course, most of those people came streaming back to the Panthers when they earned a trip to the 1996 Stanley Cup finals. Fans have short memories when the teams they root for are winners. "Now we're back to over twelve thousand season-ticket holders in a fourteen-thousand-seat building," says Torrey. "As of the start of the 1996 season, we'd sold out eleven of our first thirteen home games. There's not a ticket to be had."

Even barring the labor problems, being an NHL player is not all fun and games. The travel is grueling, especially for West Coast teams, who often have to leave the Pacific time zone to play their nearest rivals. Weeks at a time are spent away from family and friends, and loneliness is often a player's full-time companion.

Kevin Haller, a defenseman for four NHL teams said he felt lonely for years when he first broke into the NHL with Buffalo because he didn't drink or party like many of his teammates did. That made Haller a loner at a time when he needed and wanted relationships with his teammates. Over time, however, as Haller and his teammates matured, married, and started families, Haller became more comfortable.

"A lot of times it was kind of boring for me," Haller said of his early days. "I didn't go out with the other single guys, so it was all hockey for me. Now I have a wife and a couple kids and there are lots of guys on my team who are married with young kids. We get together and have fun. Getting to know the families of my teammates makes playing hockey with them all that much more fun."

Thanks to the new labor deal hammered out in 1995 between NHL commissioner Gary Bettman and Bob Goodenow, the head of the NHL Players' Association, and to the general prosperity of the league, the NHL was able to announce in June 1996 that it was accepting applications for expansion teams. Although the league had no set plans regarding potential cities for the new teams, the number of new teams to be admitted, or a timetable for their entrance into the league, Bettman was optimistic about growth. As grounds for his enthusiasm, he cited the number of applications he had received and the success, both on the ice and at the gate, of recent expansion teams in Florida, the San Jose Sharks, Anaheim Mighty Ducks, and Tampa Bay Lightning. As of the beginning of the 1997-98 season, the league had expanded in three straight years in the 1990s: San Jose had joined in 1991, Ottawa and Tampa Bay in 1992, and Florida and Anaheim in 1993.

Said Bettman in making the announcement, "Our ultimate goal will be to have new teams that will be both competitively and economically successful, that will add to our fan base, and that will enhance the NHL's position in the sports and entertainment marketplace." And Bettman, an organizational whiz who was hired by the NHL after working for years with the NBA, isn't alone in trying to jazz up the NHL—television producers are getting into the act. The Fox Network introduced the glowing puck at the 1996 All-Star Game in Boston, and hockey coverage, because of the league's growth, has been beefed up in almost every NHL city.

With young stars, such as New Jersey Devils goaltender Martin Brodeur, reaching their prime, the NHL has an attractive future.

The 1995–96 season was a banner year for the NHL. After missing all of 1994–95 because of illness and injuries, superstar center Mario Lemieux of the Pittsburgh Penguins returned to the ice and won the Hart Trophy as the league's most valuable player. The Detroit Red Wings won a record 62 regular-season games, and new arenas in Chicago, St. Louis, Boston, and Montreal ushered in an era of luxury boxes and high-tech entertainment. To cash in on all these happenings, the NHL produced a half dozen videos highlighting the season. Hockey may not have approached the other major sports in television and video exposure, but it is making up ground fast. According to the NHL, TV ratings soared for the 1996 playoffs and arenas around the league were filled to 99.6 percent capacity.

According to USA Hockey, the governing body of hockey in the United States, participation in the game on the ice grew 182 percent from 1991 to 1995. Things even looked good off the ice. According to the National Sporting Goods Association, roller hockey was the number one growth sport in the United States in 1996. Ice hockey was second.

"We had a survey presented to us at a Board of Governors meeting in New York that said that hockey, among young age groups, was considered the 'cool new game,'" says Bill Torrey. "It said that kids were flocking to it because they love being on skates. They love playing it in the street. That's fantastic." But there are problems, he says. "If we price the tickets to a point where they can't afford it, sooner or later we're going to have a leveling off and a turnaway from it. To keep growing in the United States, we have to find an economic balance. That's our biggest problem. I don't begrudge the players for the money that they get. But I don't want to see them price us to a point where in the long run we all lose."

You have to face it, fans in San Jose are proud of their team. The expansion Sharks made it to the Western Conference semifinals in 1994 and 1995.

Torrey suggests that clubs offer cheaper tickets to keep kids coming to the arenas. In Florida the Panthers reserved 900 seats per game and sold them on game day for $9 each. That kept the kids who can't afford to pay $60 for a seat coming to the games. "There are a lot of good things about the game today, and there is a lot I'm concerned about," says Torrey. "I think there are a lot more positives than negatives. There is a lot more opportunity for work these days. Any time an industry creates more opportunity, it's healthy. My concern long term is that we're pricing the game away from what should be our future. Today it's tough for kids to play our game. Kids love to play our game, but I hear it all the time: 'It's $600 or $1,000 for my kid to play.' To go to a game, tickets in Boston average over $50. Well, if we're trying to bring youth to our game and more fans and develop that core, it's pretty tough to do that with these prices. Someone asked me the other day what my first payroll was in the first year I managed. If my memory is correct, it was right around $385,000. Today you can hardly sign one player for that. We have teams now in excess of $30 million."

In 1998, the NHL shut down for two weeks so its players could compete in the Winter Olympic Games in Nagano, Japan. The Czech Republic, inspired by goaltender Dominik "The Dominator" Hasek, beat the Russians for the gold medal.

There is constant tension on the players' bench, especially when the score is tied and time is running out. Here, the Phoenix Coyotes watch the action in 1996.

Costs and participation in the league are not the only factors that have undergone changes or been the subject of scrutiny in recent years. With the growth of the league, adminstration has also become an issue. The NHL had five presidents before Gary Bettman became its first commissioner on February 1, 1993: Frank Calder (1917–1943), Mervyn "Red" Dutton (1943–1946), Clarence Campbell (1946–1977), John Ziegler (1977–1992), and Gil Stein (1992–1993).

"It's an inarguable and undeniable fact that hiring Gary Bettman has been the single most important decision that the NHL has made in its entire history," says Brian Burke. "What he accomplished in less than four years is mind-boggling. The growth that the league has undergone under his leadership is amazing. He's incredibly bright. He works like a dog. He has great vision. He's always looking ahead and saying, 'Where do we go next?' It's been a great learning experience to work for him." In 1996, three years after Bettman took office, the NHL was eighty years old, and despite some bumps along the way, was in good hands.

"Gary Bettman's blueprint so far has been a really intelligent one, and he's executed it perfectly," says Burke. "With the World Cup and the pros in the Olympics, we're looking at NHL-quality hockey being seen in every living room in North America and all over the world. The expansion to the sun belt and relocation of a couple of franchises to major markets have changed the footprint that we have on the map. Our corporate marketing strategy and the broadcast strategy have been executed. We're on network TV. The results can be seen. Ratings are up dramatically on TV. We virtually created a market in Florida that didn't exist. We added the Dallas market and the Phoenix market. It's all been positive in where the league is going."

And more expansion is on the way. "It's inevitable," says Burke. "There are some markets where we should have teams. I think the player pool will support expansion."

The World Hockey Association

t he National Hockey League saw its first true North American rival come to life in 1972. The World Hockey Association was created by Gary Davidson and Dennis Murphy, two businessmen from California who hoped to cash in on the ever-increasing popularity of the game. At its height in 1975, the WHA featured fourteen teams in locations stretching from Quebec to Houston. What really made the fledgling league a success while competing against the powerful NHL was the defection of thirty-three-year-old Bobby Hull from the NHL's Chicago Blackhawks to the WHA's Winnipeg Jets and the move of forty-six-year-old Gordie Howe from retirement to the Houston Aeros. The Jets, who eventually entered the NHL when the WHA folded in 1979, lured Hull with a job as coach and player and a salary of $2.75 million. Howe, however, was mostly attracted by the opportunity to play with his sons, Mark and Marty. They played their first game together on September 25, 1973. As he had been in the NHL, Howe was a huge success with the Aeros. He was named the league's Most Valuable Player in 1974, as he racked up 31 goals and 69 assists, and lead Houston to the Avco Cup title.

The World Hockey Association got a big boost in 1973 when Gordie Howe (left) and his sons, Marty (center) and Mark, played together for the Houston Aeros. Mark Howe went on to play sixteen seasons in the NHL.

Other star players followed Hull and Howe. Gerry Cheevers, Frank Mahovlich, and Derek Sanderson also gave credibility to the new league when they made the jump. Two future NHL coaches, Rick Ley and Ted Green, helped the Hartford Whalers win the first WHA title in 1973. In 1975, the WHA seemed destined for success. It had grown into a fourteen-team, three-division league and attendance had nearly doubled from the season before. Bobby Hull shocked the hockey world by scoring 77 goals in 78 games, and San Diego's Andre Lacroix had 106 assists. But the Aeros won their second straight championship.

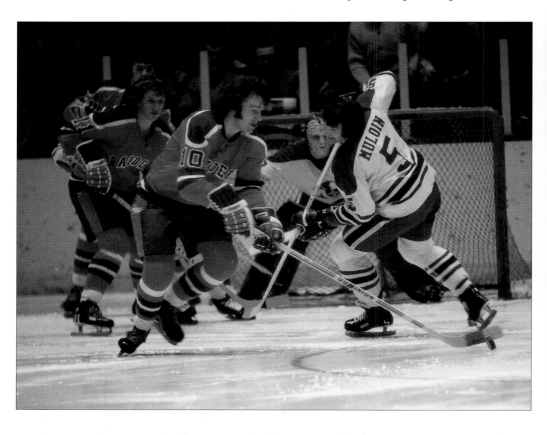

Like many players who began their careers in the NHL, John Muloin found another home in the World Hockey Association. Cleveland's 5-foot-8 (170cm), 176 pound (79kg) defenseman protects his goal against the New York Raiders.

In 1976, however, the league ran back into troubled waters. Money problems caused two teams—the Minnesota Fighting Saints and the Denver Spurs—to drop out of the league. Prospects brightened briefly in 1977 when the WHA talked the NHL into playing a 21-game exhibition and won, 13-6-2. Quebec won the championship that season, and the Howe family relocated to the Hartford franchise. The beginning of the end seemed to be at hand in 1978. The New York Rangers lured Anders Hedberg and Ulf Nilsson away from the Jets, and only eight teams managed to have enough money at the start of the season to play games. Winnipeg won the title.

The WHA's last season, 1978–79, saw just six teams ready to open the season, so league officials seriously began to entertain offers from the NHL for a merger. It was this season that Nelson Skalbania, the owner of the Indianapolis Racers, signed 17-year-old Wayne Gretzky to a personal services contract. Days before the Racers folded, Skalbania sold Gretzky's rights to Peter Pocklington and the Edmonton Oilers, and the game's greatest scorer was on his way. Gretzky later signed a 20-year deal with Edmonton and went with the Oilers when they merged into the NHL. In the final championship series, Winnipeg beat Gretzky and the Oilers in five games.

When the WHA finally went under after the 1978–79 season, four teams—the Jets, Oilers, Nordiques, and Whalers—joined the NHL.

The Junior Leagues and College Hockey

t o keep the flow of young players streaming into the league, the NHL pays millions of dollars every season to the three major leagues that make up the Canadian Hockey League. Commonly called junior hockey, these three leagues—the Ontario Hockey League, the Quebec Major Junior Hockey League, and the Western Hockey League—prepare teenage players for the rigors of the NHL.

"We have a very large financial commitment to the junior leagues," says Brian Burke. "The NHL pays them a lot of money because they provide fifty-five percent of our players, and the bulk of our stars have come through juniors. Junior hockey gives a kid at that age the best venue. That's not to say there is anything wrong with high school hockey or prep school hockey or college hockey. But in terms of pure hockey development at age seventeen or eighteen, for a kid to be able to go and play in that number of games with that level of intensity—it's clearly the fastest track to the NHL."

As is true with the minor leagues in baseball, most North American players pass through hockey's junior leagues on their way to the big time. Ed Jovanovski, a star defenseman for the Florida Panthers, was the first overall pick in the 1994 draft. He went to training camp with the Panthers in 1994 but found that he needed another season of junior hockey to hone his skills. So he went back to play one more season for the Windsor Spitfires in the Ontario Hockey League, and said afterward that it was the best thing he could have done.

"I could see I just wasn't ready," says Jovanovski, who had 10 goals and 11 assists and made the NHL all-rookie team in 1996. "One more year of junior really helped me a lot. It made me more patient and poised, and that's a hard thing to learn. You have to play relaxed in the NHL. You have to play with a lot of enthusiasm, but you have to let things come to you and not force them. There is no pressure on you in juniors. You're out there to learn from your mistakes. That's a big part of coaching there. You let guys make mistakes and then throw them back out there to learn from them."

Some hockey people think that junior hockey is rated too highly over college hockey. Ron Wilson, coach of the Washington Capitals, Team USA in the 1996 World Cup, and the 1998 U.S. Olympic team, says that college hockey can prepare players just as well, if not better, than the junior leagues. Wilson,

Even as a junior-league player, Eric Lindros had a powerful slapshot. He scored 71 goals in 57 games in the 1990-91 season for the Oshawa Generals.

a defenseman, was a two-time All-American at Providence College and the Hockey East Player of the Year in 1975. He went on to play for Toronto and Minnesota in the NHL, scoring 93 points in 177 games.

"A lot of the better kids are told that junior hockey is better, so they go and play junior," says Wilson. "It's not so much that the development there is better, but the kids with talent go play junior more so than they go to college."

However, Wilson says, some college programs outperform the junior teams. "You practice a lot more in college and in the long run you're better off for it," Wilson says. "We stress playing games too often when practice and off-ice work-outs are just as good. Brian Leetch went one year and played at Boston College. Can you say that Boston College created Brian Leetch? No. Joe Sakic played junior hockey. Did junior hockey create Joe Sakic? No. Either way, they're going to be great hockey players. It's not fair to compare. In college, getting an education is very important, and that's a factor that is missed in junior hockey.

Before they reach the pros, players in junior and college hockey learn to use their elbows and knees to jostle along the boards.

"You come out of college a little more mature. You come into the NHL at twenty, twenty-one, twenty-two. Juniors generally come in at eighteen or nineteen, and they're not quite ready. There is a maturity factor. I like the NBA system where kids are drafted from college programs. Look at the NBA. The college programs play thirty, thirty-five games. They don't play eighty games. Michael Jordan didn't have to play eighty games in college to get ready for the NBA. He went to college. He matured. He practiced a lot. The NBA also has summer leagues, and they do a lot in basketball that we don't even attempt to do in hockey."

The U.S. college programs, which play under the the auspices of the National Collegiate Athletic Association, are filled with players from both the United States and Canada. The NCAA, which sponsors national championships in three divisions, held its first tournament in 1948 and has sent hundreds of talented players into both the NHL and various Olympic programs. The Association is in turn divided into the Central Collegiate Hockey Association, the Eastern College Athletic Conference, Hockey East and the Western Collegiate Hockey Association. Among the best college programs are those at Michigan, Boston University, Lake Superior State, Wisconsin, Harvard, North Dakota, Maine, Providence, and Minnesota.

The American Hockey League

t he American Hockey League celebrated its sixtieth anniversary in 1996. Designed as a developmental league for the NHL, the AHL enjoyed its best season in 1995–1996. In that season, twenty of the NHL's twenty-six teams used the AHL as their developmental league. According to the AHL, 62 percent of all players in the NHL had passed through the AHL on their way to the big show.

The AHL also boasts a program that advances referees and linesmen from the minor league to the NHL. Of course, coaches also gain valuable experience in working for AHL teams before moving on to the NHL. A recent example of an AHL coach making the successful transition was in 1996 when Marc Crawford, the former coach of the St. John's Maple Leafs, won the Stanley Cup with the Colorado Avalanche.

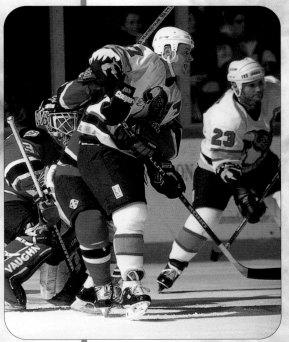

The eight original franchises of the AHL were the Providence Rhode Island Reds, New Haven Eagles, Philadelphia Ramblers, Springfield Indians, Syracuse Stars, Pittsburgh Hornets, Cleveland Barons, and Buffalo Bison. Syracuse won the first championship trophy, called the Calder Cup, which was named after Frank Calder, the NHL's first president. In 1995, the AHL reached the 3 million mark in attendance for the first time, and its average of 4,942 fans per game was its highest average ever.

Other successful alumni include Tim Horton, the winner of four Stanley Cup rings and a Hockey Hall of Famer; Larry Robinson, a six-time Stanley Cup winner and another Hall of Famer, Brett Hull, the Hart Trophy winner at the NHL's most valuable player; and Mike Keenan, coach of the 1994 Stanley Cup champion New York Rangers.

Two Springfield Falcons set up in front of the net. The Falcons joined the AHL in 1994 and served as the farm team for the Hartford Whalers and Winnipeg Jets.

There are other minor leagues, as well. They include the International Hockey League, the East Coast Hockey League, the Colonial Hockey League, the Central Hockey League, and the Southern Hockey League. These leagues differ from the junior leagues in that the players earn salaries. Junior-league players are considered amateurs.

The All-Star Game

The NHL All-Star Game is exciting for fans because they have been permitted in recent years to vote for the two six-player starting lineups. The 1998 season marked the thirteenth year in which the fans had voted. Players are selected to represent the Western and Eastern conferences. Twenty centers, thirty-six left and right wingers, thirty-six defensemen, and twenty goalies are on the ballots each season. Every team in the league has at least one representative in the voting pool. Although the three days off during the All-Star break are welcomed by many players, being voted to or named as a team member is a great honor for most players.

"It's great to play with the other guys who are in the Game," says Eric Lindros, a four-time All-Star through 1998. "How often do you see hockey talent like this all in one room?"

On January 20, 1996, in one of the most dramatic games in All-Star Game history, Boston defenseman Raymond Bourque, with just 15 seconds left to play, scored the winning goal in front of his hometown fans at Boston's new Fleet Center. That goal lifted the Eastern Conference to a 5–4 victory over the Western Conference. Because of the goal, Bourque was named the game's most valuable player.

Goaltender Chris Osgood got into this predicament in the 1996 All-Star Game. Defenseman Al MacInnis, caught out of position, tries to help out.

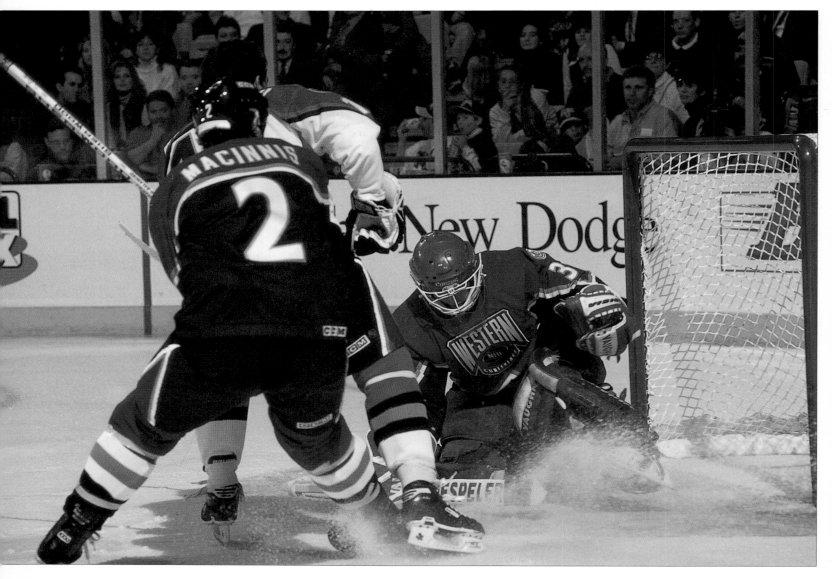

The 1996 All-Star Game was at Boston's new Fleet Center, and 17,565 fans saw the dramatic ending.

Like the Stanley Cup playoffs, the All-Star Game has a colorful history full of exciting games and memorable heroes. When the Game first began, it wasn't played between the two conferences. In 1947, a collection of All-Stars from the entire league played the first official game against the defending Cup champions, the Toronto Maple Leafs. The All-Stars were coached by Montreal's Dick Irvin and selected by hockey broadcasters and writers. Hap Day was the head man of the Maple Leafs, and twenty-three representative of the press applied for credentials. These days, hundreds of reporters cover the game, and it's shown live in Canada and the United States on national television.

There are dozens of All-Star heroes. Toronto winger Vincent Damphousse tied the All-Star Game record by scoring 4 goals in 1991 in Chicago to lead the Campbell Conference over the Wales Conference, 11-5. Mario Lemieux scored 4 goals in front of his hometown fans at Pittsburgh's Civic Arena in 1990 to lead the Wales past the Campbell, 12–7. Lemieux was also honored before the 1993 Game in Montreal, which he had to miss because he was suffering from Hodgkins Disease. Los Angeles Kings star Wayne Gretzky returned to Edmonton in 1989 for his first All-Star Game since being traded by the Oilers and won his second MVP award by recording a goal and 2 assists. In 1988, Lemeiux scored a record 6 points and Montreal winger Mats Naslund had a record 5 assists as the Wales Conference beat the Campbell Conference, 6-5. Detroit's Gordie Howe, who played in a record 23 All-Star Games, played in his fourteenth straight in 1971 to break Maurice Richard's mark of thirteen straight appearances.

In 1993, Mike Gartner got a chance to play in the All-Star Game in Montreal because Mark Messier was injured. After Gartner scored 4 goals to win the MVP Award and the accompanying new car, he was asked whether he owed Messier anything. Gartner said he owed Messier a handshake, but that he would keep the car. In the age catagory, Detroit's Steve Yzerman is the youngest player not on a Cup championship team to have played in an All-Star Game. Yzerman's age was eighteen years, eight months, and twenty-two days when he played for the Campbell Conference in 1984.

Vancouver Canucks
goalie John Garrett
gets caught out of
position in the 1983
All-Star Game at
Nassau Coliseum in
Uniondale, NY.

Things even percolated off the ice at the 1962 Game in Toronto. Star left winger Frank Mahovlich was seeking a new contract from the Maple Leafs, but a few hours before the game the Chicago Blackhawks tried to buy Mahovlich from Toronto for $1 million. The Leafs eventually turned down the offer and signed their best player to a four-year deal that was worth nearly as much.

Goaltenders have had their share of All-Star glory, too. Montreal's Charlie Hodge and Gary Bauman shut out the dynamic line of Gordie Howe, Stan Mikita, and Bobby Hull in a memorable 3–0 victory in 1967. Goalies for the Canadiens in 1957 weren't so lucky. Detroit's Production Line, broken up when Ted Lindsay was traded before the season, was reunited at the Montreal Forum. Howe, Lindsay, and Alex Delvecchio played together again, and Howe scored a power-play goal in the All-Stars' 5–3 victory. As for coaches, Tommy Ivan, vice president of the Chicago Blackhawks in 1996, is the only coach with at least four All-Star appearances to go undefeated. Ivan, the former coach of the Blackhawks, was 3–0–1 in appearances in 1948, 1949, 1950, and 1952.

All-Star Games have been sprinkled with controversies. Because coaches chose the players in the early games—fans vote for the starters these days and a general managers' committee chooses the reserves—there was often disagreement about the selections. Montreal's Dick Irvin created a stir in 1951 when he selected his own goalie, Gerry McNeil, instead of Toronto's Al Rollins who had won the Vezina Trophy the season before. It was the first time the Vezina Trophy winner of the previous season did not play in the All-Star Game. In the end, McNeil showed he was deserving of the honor by allowing just one goal in 30 minutes of play as the First Team All-Stars tied the Second Team All-Stars, 2–2.

A similar incident took place at the 1972 Game. Chicago coach Billy Reay chose Blackhawks Keith Magnuson and Pit Martin instead of Minnesota's Murray Oliver to give the Hawks a record nine players on the West team. Minnesota general manager Wren Blair was so upset about the slight to Oliver that he proposed taking the responsibility of selecting the players away from the coaches. The motion was denied. Of course the task of selecting the reserves was finally given to a committee of general managers in 1992.

There has also been tragedy at the games. The 1968 All-Star Game was a sad affair as Minnesota center Bill Masterton had died on January 15, a day before the game, from head injuries he sustained in a game against the Oakland Seals just two days earlier. Toronto's Brian Conacher responded by being the first player to wear a helmet in an All-Star Game. Later that season, the league created the Bill Masterton Memorial Trophy, an annual award given by the Professional Hockey Writers Assocation and presented to the NHL player "who best exemplifies the qualities of perseverance, sportsmanship and dedication to hockey" during the regular season. A $2,500 grant from the association is awarded to a scholarship fund in Bloomington, Minnesota in the name of the winner. Winger Gary Roberts of the Calgary Flames won the 1996 award for returning to action after being sidelined for eleven months after two major surgeries, which were the result of a cervical neck injury.

There were three "unofficial" All-Star Games played before the "official" game was played in 1947. All three were organized to honor NHL players who had died or been injured. Excited fans filled Maple Leaf Gardens on February 14, 1934 when the league held a benefit game between the Stanley Cup champion Maple Leafs and a squad of NHL All-Stars. The game benefitted Irvine "Ace" Bailey and raised over $23,000. Bailey was a former Maple Leaf left winger who suffered a fractured skull in 1933 after being checked by Eddie Shore, a defenseman for the Boston Bruins. Bailey was forced to retire shortly after the incident, and NHL president Frank Calder, Toronto owner Conn Smythe, and Montreal owner Leo Dandurand organized the benefit. Shore, in an emotional gesture before the game, skated out to center ice and shook hands with Bailey. The Maple Leafs went on to defeat Shore and his All-Star teamates, 7–3.

Hall of Famer Howie Morenz was honored in an All-Star Game in Montreal on November 3, 1937. Morenz had died at the age of thirty-four of heart failure as a result of complications from a broken leg he suffered in a game. The All-Stars won that game, 6–5, over a team comprised of Canadiens and Montreal Maroons, as more than $20,000 was raised for Morenz's family.

The third tribute All-Star game was played on October 29, 1939, and it was called the Babe Siebert Memorial Game. Albert Charles Siebert, known as "Babe," had been named coach of the Canadiens in the summer of 1939, but drowned shortly thereafter and Pit Lepine became the Montreal coach. The next season, Dick Irvin would take over the Canadiens and coach until 1955. In raising $15,000 for Siebert's widow and children, a team of All-Stars tripped the host Canadiens, 5–2.

Over the seasons, the NHL has tinkered with the game to make it more attractive to fans and more exciting for the players. Until 1967, the game was played at the beginning of the regular season and not, as it is today, at the halfway point. Through 1950, the defending Cup champions had played an all-star team. But in 1951, the league shook things up. Stan Saplin, publicity director for the New York Rangers, is credited with suggesting that two All-Star teams be created to play one another. So, for two seasons the First Team All-Stars, comprised of players from the four U.S.-based teams—New York, Boston, Chicago, and Detroit—played the Second Team All-Stars, which consisted of players from the two Canadian-based teams—Toronto and Montreal. Apparently, the change was a dud. The two games ended in low-scoring ties—2–2 and 1–1—so the league went back to the old format of the All-Stars against the Cup champions.

Even in those days, the game of hockey competed against baseball and football for space in the sports pages and time on the broadcast reports. With the All-Star game being played in October, it was competing for publicity against baseball's World Series and the big games in college and professional football. So in 1967, following the suggestion of Art Ross, who had first voiced the idea in 1951, the league moved the All-Star to the middle of the season in January. Actually, Ross wanted the game to be played on the American holiday of Thanksgiving, but by the time the change was made, the league had expanded, and the schedule was much longer.

The custom of the defending Cup champions playing against an All-Star team lasted until 1969. Two years previously, the league had expanded to twelve teams and divided into East and West Divisions. The divisions chose their own

Above: Tim Horton (7) can't keep Alex Delvecchio (10) from getting one past Johnny Bower in the 1962 All-Star game.

Opposite: Winger Daniel Alfredsson gets his stick up high on defenseman Derian Hatcher at the 1997 All-Star Game in San Jose.

All-Stars and faced off in the general format that is used today. That game ended in a 3–3 tie and was the first in another area, as well. Players on the winning team received $500 each while players on the losing team received $250.

The Wales Conference and Campbell Conference were created in 1974, and their All-Star teams faced off for the first time in 1975. In 1990, the NHL created an All-Star Game weekend format and added a Heroes of Hockey Game and skills competition. The Heroes game, played by retired stars, and the skills competition, held for active players, are held on the Friday before the game. The All-Star Game is played on Saturday. To honor long service to the NHL, two active veteran players were permitted to be added to the All-Star team rosters in 1991. Guy Lefleur skated with the Wales Conference, and Bobby Smith played for the Campbell Conference that first year. The Wales Conference won 12 of the first 17 All-Star Games they played, including a 16–6 whitewash in 1993 in Montreal that marked the last All-Star Game to be played at the Forum. In 1996, the Canadiens moved to the new Molson Center. In the 1993 skills compeition, defenseman Al Iafrate won the slapshot competition with a shot of 105.2 miles per hour.

In 1994, the conferences became the Eastern and Western, and the Eastern won in Boston in 1996. The 1995 game was not held because of the lockout that shut the league down for the first half of the season. The East beat the West in the 1997 All-Star Game in San Jose, and North America beat the World's All-Stars in the 1998 Game in Vancouver.

Wayne Gretzky maneuvers around Al Maccinnis in the 1997 All-Star game.

The Rinks

One of the most important inventions in the development of hockey was artificial ice. Since early games had to be played on natural ice, the players were at the mercy of the elements. If a sudden heat wave appeared, the game had to be cancelled or, at least, postponed until the temperatures dropped.

Artificial ice began to appear in rinks in the early 1920s. Of course, those rinks were crude predecessors to today's modern rinks. Today's refrigeration systems are a wonder of modern technology. To make the ice for the 200-foot by 85-foot (61m × 26m) rinks, arena engineers utilize huge chilling systems that weigh several tons. The CoreStates Center, which opened in Philadelphia at the start of the 1996–97 season, uses three 1,000-ton (907–metric ton) chillers to keep the arena cool during the summer months and three 150-ton (136–metric ton) chillers to make the ice.

To make the rink, the temperature of the arena is lowered to 61°F (16° C). Antifreeze is fed into pipes that are laid an inch and a half (3.7cm) below the frozen concrete floor of the rink. Through this, a layer of frost develops on the top of the concrete. Several layers of water are poured on top of the frost, and white paint is applied to give the ice color. More water is added to make the ice thicker, and the lines, circles and logos are painted on top of that. A quarter inch (1.8cm) of ice is frozen on top of everything to complete the process.

The Zamboni, the huge machine that cleans the ice, was first used in the late 1940s when resurfacing between periods became mandatory.

Overall, it takes 10,000 gallons (38,000l) of water and two and a half days to make an inch of ice.

The Big Four

"The records are nice, but if you're not winning you're not having fun."

WAYNE GRETZKY,
New York Rangers

In spite of our best efforts to keep life orderly and predictable, sometimes something or somebody comes along that turns our world upside down. Wayne Gretzky, Bobby Orr, Gordie Howe, and Mario Lemieux did that in the hockey world. There certainly were stars before these four players left their imprint on the history of hockey, and the game would have gone along just fine without them. But it wouldn't have had the grace, beauty, and superior achievements that these four players have contributed. Not only did these four players rack up records and win championships for their teams, they also inspired whole generations to take up hockey sticks and hit the local lakes, ponds, and rinks. The National Hockey League, forever battling football, baseball, and basketball for space in the crowded world of professional sports, needed super-stars like these four to make it popular with the fans. It also needed them to give young players models to emulate; idols to dream about.

Wayne Gretzky

Wayne Gretzky moves like a ghost on the ice. Now he's in the corner with the puck. Now he's behind the net sizing up Mark Messier or Jari Kurri or Rick Tocchet in the slot. Now he's passing the puck and a teammate is scoring. "He's so good you have to be careful you don't get caught watching him play while you're on the ice, too," says center Craig MacTavish, a teammate of Gretzky in the glory days of the Edmonton Oilers.

Arguably the most talented player ever to put stick to puck, Gretzky has made many additions to the record books. The Great One, a nickname he earned as a young player who could outscore entire teams at a time, went into the 1997-98 season as the NHL's all-time leading scorer, with 862 goals and 1,843 assists. Playing nineteen seasons for the Edmonton Oilers, Los Angeles Kings, and St. Louis Blues, Gretzky, who signed as a free agent with the New York Rangers in 1996, owns or shares sixty-one NHL records. He won the Hart Trophy as the league's most valuable player nine times, the Art Ross Trophy as the leading scor-er ten times, the Lady Byng Trophy as the most gentlemanly and outstanding player four times, and the Conn Smythe Trophy as the most valuable player of the playoffs twice.

"When you're getting chances, eventually good things happen," says Gretzky. "You just have to keep working hard. There are no secrets in this game....The only thing that pays off is hard work. If you work hard and are still creating chances and opportunities, eventually the puck will go into the net."

Hockey experts marvel at how Wayne Gretzky "sees" the ice. His ability to anticipate the play and position himself to score makes him arguably the greatest player ever.

In becoming the most famous hockey player ever, Gretzky also became a spokesman for the game. He hosted television shows and married an actress. His pictures are sprinkled throughout popular culture magazines, as well as through the sports sections of major newspapers around North America. He is one of the few players who transcends sports and is famous for his popularity as well as his achievements.

"The biggest thing for me when I'm around the guys is I don't expect to be treated any differently than anybody else," says Gretzky. "I'm one of the guys, whether it's to razz somebody or be razzed. I think sometimes people get on their heels around me. With Mark Messier there with me on the Rangers, right off the bat people knew that I'm just one of the guys. It made me more comfortable."

It didn't take long for Gretzky to show that he was going to dominate the NHL like no one before him. He became a pro with the Indianapolis Racers in the World Hockey Association when he was just seventeen, and although he was never the physically strongest player on the ice he dominated game after game. He moved to the Oilers when the Racers folded and almost immediately began to make hockey history when Edmonton joined the NHL in 1979. Showing a pizzazz with the puck (his stickhandling made him a threat to pass or shoot whenever he touched the puck), Gretzky began to overtake every scoring record in the books. He scored an incredible record 92 goals and scored 212 points in the 1981–82 season. He piled up 163 assists and 215 points in 1985–86, and he led the Oilers to four Stanley Cup championships.

"Gretzky probably doesn't stickhandle as well as Mario Lemieux, but he anticipates the play better than anybody I've ever seen," says Joe Watson, who played fourteen NHL seasons with Boston, Philadelphia, and Colorado. "Sometimes you watch him play and he skates away from everybody and you wonder where the heck he's going. Suddenly, the puck winds up where he is, and you say, 'How did he know the

Gretzky scored 12 goals in the 1987–88 playoffs, and led the Oilers to victory over goalie Reggie Lemelin and the Boston Bruins in the Stanley Cup finals.

puck was going to go there?' He just knows what is going to happen before the rest of us."

"You always have to be aware of where he is on the ice," says Gary Dornhoefer, who played fourteen NHL seasons with Boston and Philadelphia. "Before Gretzky, you always knew where the forwards would be. But he is so quick to skate out of the defensive zone that you have to actually stand right beside him to know where he is. I think he'll do great in New York because he'll be inspired by Mark Messier."

On August 9, 1988, in a trade that would change the face of the NHL, Oilers owner Peter Pocklington traded Gretzky and two other players to the Los Angeles Kings for two players, three first-round draft picks, and $15 million. That trade, designed to bolster Pocklington's troubled financial prospects, also bolstered hockey along the Pacific Coast Highway. In leading the Kings to the 1993 Stanley Cup finals, Gretzky also became the veteran spokesman for the league. Near the end of the 1995–96 season Gretzky, facing total free agency, was traded to St. Louis. The next two seasons, 1996-97 and 1997-98, he played for the New York Rangers. Criticized by some for being selfish and manipulative of management as his fame and fortune grew, Gretzky has nonetheless became the most famous and successful NHL player ever. He surpassed Gordie Howe's career record of 1,850 points on October 15, 1989, when he scored a goal to tie a game against Edmonton with just 53 seconds left in regulation play. It was only fitting then that Gretzky also scored the winning goal in overtime.

"Winning is what I've tried to point to throughout my career," says Gretzky. "I've played with some great players on some great teams. But winning is what the game is about."

Left winger Pat Conacher played with Gretzky in both Edmonton and Los Angeles. "He's been the greatest player *in* the game and the greatest player *for* the game," Conacher says. "Away from the game, he's one of the greatest people I've ever met. People try to find dirt on him all the time. There is no dirt. Unfortunately, he's always being compared to himself. It's unfair. Who is ever going to get 215 points or score 92 goals again? No one. Somewhere down the road someone may come and do it. But I doubt it.

"He carried the league for so many years. Let's face it. Florida, San Jose, Anaheim, even the Kings—none of those teams would be there if not for Gretzky. Go anywhere and they know who Wayne Gretzky is. He played in Edmonton, Alberta, the smallest market in the league, and his name in everywhere, not only in North America but in Europe."

Conacher accompanied Gretzky on a tour of Europe in 1994 and couldn't believe how popular Gretzky was. He said he found out that the Oilers were considered to be "Europe's team" when Gretzky and Jari Kurri were leading them to Cups in the 1980s.

"It really opened my eyes to just how big Wayne Gretzky was," Conacher says. "The thing is, he's had the longevity. And every night he came out and cared about where the game was going and how he could create. I think that was just natural. It was the competitive spirit in his heart. He really cared about the game. He has a love for it, a passion, like no one else. You could talk to Wayne Gretzky in the dressing room and ask him any question about the early 1900s on. He'll tell you goal scorers and anything you want to know. That's one of the reasons he's such a great player."

Bobby Orr

Bobby Orr was a revolutionary in more ways than one. A great skater who could pass and handle the puck as well, if not better, than anyone in the 1970s, Orr revolutionized the play of defensemen. Along with his agent, Alan Eagleson, who later was disgraced for his mishandling of the players' association finances, Orr also forced the Boston Bruins to pay him the then-staggering sum of $40,000 a year. On the ice, Orr placed greater emphasis on scoring goals than stopping them, and he rocketed to fame by becoming the first defenseman to lead the NHL in scoring. Like Eddie Shore before him, Orr loved to carry the puck up the ice and fire it at the goaltender. And while he was criticized for not paying enough attention to his defensive responsibilities, no one could question his ability to skate and score. He won 8 consecutive Norris Trophies as the NHL's best defenseman.

Bobby Orr loved to skate the length of the ice and fire shots at surprised goaltenders. He scored 46 goals in the 1974-75 season.

"He was the finest player to ever lace his skates on," says Joe Watson, who broke in with the Bruins just before Orr. "When you think of players controlling the game you think of forwards. But Orr, because he was a defenseman and had to play both ends of the rink, controlled the game more than any other player ever. He'd set plays up, score himself, and still play in his own end."

In 1970 Orr became the first player to win four individual trophies in the same year. He won the Hart Trophy as the league's most valuable player, the Norris Trophy as the best defenseman, the Art Ross Trophy as the scoring leader, and the Conn Smythe Trophy as the playoff MVP. Orr also scored an acrobatic goal in Game Four of the 1970 finals against the St. Louis Blues to give the Bruins their first Cup since 1941. In 1996 that play was voted by a panel of 400 writers and broadcasters as the greatest moment in NHL history. Eventually, bad knees forced Orr out of hockey. After half a dozen operations, the player who changed the way defensemen played in the NHL retired at the age of thirty.

"He was a player in his own class, all by himself," says Hall of Famer Bill Barber. "There is no other Bobby Orr today. You've got Brian Leetch and Chris Chelios, but there is only one Bobby Orr."

"I hate to say it, but I spent more time watching him than I did playing against him, and I was on the ice," says Gary Dornhoefer. "He would literally mesmerize other players. He was the one player who could turn the pace of the game into his pace. He was certainly the best player in hockey during his time. It's such a shame that his injuries ended his career. I would have loved to see what kind of numbers he could have put up."

"Players who have had impact are players who have changed the game," says Bill Torrey, president of the Florida Panthers. "Bobby Orr was not only a great player; he had impact on the game and changed it."

"He's a wonderful person and one of the great guys," says Gerry Cheevers, a goalie with Toronto and Boston from 1961–1980. "Few guys could do it all. Bobby Orr could."

Gordie Howe

Gordie Howe, or Mr. Hockey, as he is known to millions of fans, is famous mostly for his 1,071 career goals in an era of superior defense and his amazing all-

Gordie Howe's blazing slapshot was only one element of his dominating game.

around play. But the most astounding of all the accomplishments of Howe's thirty-two-year career may be the fact that he played at all. In 1950 Howe, trying to check another player, crashed into the boards and smashed his head. Players didn't wear helmets in those days; years later, the league would recall Howe's injury and rule that all players must wear helmets. Without head protection, however, Howe was severely injured and needed surgery to relieve pressure on his brain. But amazingly he recovered in time to continue playing for the Detroit Red Wings the next season.

Howe began his career with the Wings as an eighteen-year-old from Floral, Saskatchewan. The length of his career was unheard of in any sport, let alone the bruising game of hockey; he started playing professionally in 1946 and ended his career in 1980. When he retired, Howe was fifty-one years old, a grandfather, and playing right wing in the World Hockey Association with his two sons, Mark and Marty.

Howe simply did not appear to age. When he was forty-one, Howe scored a career-best 103 points. He ended his 1,767-game NHL career with 801 goals and 1,049 assists for 1,850 points. In the 1950s, Howe and Maurice "Rocket" Richard waged some of the most pitched scoring duels in hockey. Since Howe was ambidextrous, he could shoot with either hand. Partly because of that skill, he won the Hart Trophy as the NHL's best most valuable player six times and the Art Ross Trophy as the leading scorer six times. Eventually, Howe would surpass Richard's record for most goals in a career.

"He was a big strong guy who took over games with his strength and attitude," says Joe Watson. "He was as good a passer as he was a scorer. The big thing about him, though, was his mean streak. When he got mad at you you knew it was time to move out of his way."

Unlike Gretzky, Howe was never much for playing a gentlemanly game. He liked to use his elbows and his stick to keep hounding defensemen away. Famous as the right wing on Detroit's "Production Line" of the 1940s and 1950s, Howe, who played with centers Sid Abel and Alex Delvecchio and left winger Ted Lindsay, would barrel over anyone who got in his way. He still holds the record for most penalty minutes in All-Star Game history, with 27 in 23 games. He led the Wings to the Stanley Cup finals seven times in nine seasons between 1948 and 1956 and helped them win the Cup four times.

"I played with him in 1978 in Zurich in an international series, and I got to know him pretty well," says goalie Gerry Cheevers. "He's a terrific person, and he loves to play the game. It was fun playing with him and difficult playing against him."

When Eric Lindros entered the NHL with the Flyers in 1992, he was compared to Howe on the basis of his strength, aggressive play, and scoring ability. For his part, Howe may have been mean on the ice when he roamed about with a stick, but like Gretzky after him, he was an effective spokesman for the game. Nearly twenty years after his last goal, Howe was a big draw for fans and media at NHL games and functions. Of his 1,071 goals, 801 were scored in the NHL.

Howe was named to twelve NHL first-team All-Star squads and nine second-team squads. He played in 23 All-Star Games. After sitting out three seasons to serve as a vice president for the Red Wings, Howe got the itch to play again. So he signed on with the Houston Aeros of the World Hockey League, where he showed the hockey world he could still bury the biscuit.

"The National Hockey League is almost the same age as Gordie Howe," says Brian Burke. "Not many people realize that. What Gordie contributed, what Bobby Orr contributed can never be overlooked because they are a critical part of the presence of the NHL."

Mario Lemieux

One of the most heralded players ever to come out of junior hockey and into the NHL, Mario Lemieux has lived up to every expectation anyone could have placed on him. Suffering from Hodgkin's Disease and a chronic bad back, Lemieux sat out the shortened 48-game season of 1994–95 only to return with a vengeance the following season. In 1995–96, Lemieux won his fifth scoring title by racking up 161 points on 69 goals and 92 assists; he also won the Hart Trophy as the NHL's most valuable player. In 1996–97, his last season, Lemieux scored 50 goals and won the NHL scoring title with 122 points.

"It really showed his heart," Conacher says of Lemieux's comeback. "You have to take you hat off to the guy. The courage he showed in coming back and all the things he had to go through. He's proven his critics wrong, and he's probably the best player in the NHL. He'll be one of the best ever."

Like Gretzky, Lemieux seems to be a magician with the puck. He can sneak a pass to a teammate between the skates of an opponent. He can outskate nearly anybody. He can whiz a shot from high in the slot or slip one in from behind the net. When he first entered the NHL, Lemieux appeared to be on his way to becoming the greatest player ever to play the game. He scored 100 points as a rookie and had 494 goals in his first 599 games. Thanks largely to his spectacular play, the Pittsburgh Penguins won the Stanley Cup in 1991 and 1992. As with Howe, you get caught up watching Lemieux play, says former teammate Kjell Samuelsson. "He's so valuable as an offensive player because he doesn't give the puck away," says Gary Dornhoefer. "He always makes good passes. I mean it. Always. And he makes defensemen afraid to challenge him. If you try to stop him as he's coming down the ice, chances are that he'll make you look silly, and nobody wants that. He reminds me of a chess player. He's always one step ahead of everybody else." Bob Clarke, general manager of the Philadelphia Flyers, says, "He's so consistent. He always seems to make the right decisions with the puck, and that is very rare."

The 1995–96 season wasn't even Lemieux's best. In 1988–89 he had scored 85 goals and had 114 assists for 199 points. But the 1995–96 season was rewarding for Lemieux, so much so that he elected to play only one more season before seriously considering retirement. Not only did Lemieux win the 1996 Art Ross Trophy for scoring the most points, he also was named to the first-team All-Star squad. He scored his 500th career goal in October 1995 and became the fourth player in NHL history to win the scoring title five times or more.

"Mario sees the ice better than almost anyone who ever played," says Joe Watson, who won two Stanley Cups with Philadelphia. "And he plays defense more than people think. He gets a lot of criticism for scoring all those points and not playing defense, but when he has to get back and cover his end, he does it. He's probably the best player I've ever seen shift the way he handles the puck. Most guys go at the defenseman with the puck on the right side or left side. Lemieux can shift it back and forth so fast that you can't even see it. You're looking for the puck, and wham, he's by you. You can pick up the tendencies of most players, know what they're going to do by studying them for a while. You can't do that with Lemieux."

Florida's Terry Carkner has his hands full trying to keep Mario Lemieux away from goalie John Vanbiesbrouck in the 1995–96 NHL playoffs.

Greatness Personified

"Hard work has always been
what I thought was the basic thing
for a great player."

MIKE BOSSY,
HALL OF FAME WINGER

One of the great things about hockey is that it's easy to compare players from different eras. It's not so easy to reach conclusions, though. "The game has changed," says Hall of Fame left winger Bill Barber, who along with Bobby Clarke and Reggie Leach comprised the Flyers' famous "LCB (Leach, Clarke, Barber) Line" of the 1970s. "In the old days there was no such thing as hanging out at the red line and waiting for goals. You had to come back in deep and play defense. In my era, players who were one-dimensional didn't last very long. Today, the athletes are bigger, stronger, faster. So it's hard to compare."

Because of that, there will always be arguments over which players are the best at their positions. Would Wayne Gretzky have been as effective as a passer if he had played in the 1930s, when the game was rougher? Would Gordie Howe excel in today's speed game? It's impossible to know, so the arguments will go on forever.

Still, some things are eternal. Great players always dominate their eras. Here is how some of the greatest players ever to play the game characterize greatness:

"Hard work has always been what I thought was the basic thing for a great player," says Hall of Fame winger Mike Bossy. "Obviously there are different players who have different talents and different levels of talent. But the desire to always be the best on any given night is something special that not everybody has. Confidence is a big thing, too. If you think you can do it before you have to go and do it, you have a stride on everybody else."

"Consistency is the mark of a great player," says Eric Lindros, the winner of the 1995 Hart Trophy as the NHL's most valuable player. "Being consistent at a high level over the course of your career is the most important thing a player can accomplish. In an 82-game season, obviously you're not going to be on every night. Say in your first year you're kind of hit-and-miss and you're happy with your play in 40, 45 games. Then you develop to the point where you're solid for 70 games. When that happens, you've become a guy who can be counted on in most situations.

"You can talk about great players who in the course of the regular season have 40 goals. But if only 8 of them are game winners, are they great players? A great player always wants to make great plays all the time. He's got to want to be counted on, and he has to be humble when things are going his way. A lot of times the team will reflect the personality of a great player. No one likes to walk into a building and play against a guy who is confident but who keeps things at an even keel all the time. Never getting too high or too low is an important part of it."

"Leadership is the biggest thing," says three-time All-Star right winger Theoren Fleury of the Calgary Flames. "But you've got to score and make plays. And you've got to play injured."

Losing comes hard to the best players, but they always seem to know how to bounce back. "Every team goes through its ups and downs," says star winger Jari Kurri. "Basically you have to go back to basics. Win the battles one on one. Sometimes you try to do things too hard. But you have to win your confidence back. It's not magic. You have to work hard at it and think that's it's going to happen."

When Jari Kurri's scoring production declined, he helped out the Los Angeles Kings by killing penalties and playing strong defense.

The Center

"It's a little bit of everything all over the ice."

Dale Hawerchuk,
Philadelphia Flyers

Opposite: Star center Eric Lindros entered the NHL with the Philadelphia Flyers when he was nineteen years old but quickly matured into a potent offensive force.

Below: Sergei Fedorov eyes up his adversary before the puck is dropped for a faceoff.

Iike the quarterback on a football team or a pitcher on a baseball club, the center usually dominates the action in hockey. Of course, superstars such as Wayne Gretzky and Mario Lemieux would dominate games no matter what position they played. But even the most defensive-minded centers, such as Criag MacTavish, now retired, and Sergei Fedorov of the Detroit Red Wings, play important roles for their teams.

Most coaches like their centers to be the players who distribute the puck to the wingers. The center is depended on to read the defense and determine where the weakness lies. Once he spots the point of attack, the center must either get there himself and wait for the puck or draw the defense to him so that one of his wingers can get open. And it's all got to happen in seconds. The center may not be the best player on the team. But he's got to be the most versatile and unselfish.

"A good offense through a long year is important, if for no other reason than mentally, because it's a strain when you don't score," says Mark Messier of the Vancouver Canucks. "It becomes a bit of a strain to play a tight game, game in and game out. Mistakes are magnified and everybody starts pressing."

Eric Lindros, who led the Flyers to the Stanley Cup finals in 1997, became a star by playing in between wingers John LeClair and Mikael Renberg. According

to Lindros, his job was easy because LeClair and Renberg were always hanging around the net looking for rebounds. "All I have to do is get the puck in deep and try to make a play to the front of the net," says Lindros, who racked up 68 assists in 1995–96. "Communication is always the most important thing, but knowing the other guys and what they like to do is just as important."

"The center tries to control the puck," says Dale Hawerchuk, who went into the 1997–98 season ranked twenty-first on the NHL's all-time goals list with 518. In 1995–96, Hawerchuk became just the twenty-third player in NHL history to score 500 career goals. Describing the objective of the center, he says: "He wants to draw a defender to him and hit a winger with a pass. Of course, most of his work is done through the middle of the ice. Being able to see the ice is critical. The centers most often have to create the plays, so seeing what is happening and what probably will happen is important. Defensively, since the wingers are going to cover the opposing defensemen, the center usually drops low to help the defensemen. It's a little bit of everything all over the ice."

Of all the forwards, the centers usually score the most goals. The NHL's all-time statistics are skewed a bit because Wayne Gretzky was such a dominant scorer. But the wingers, as a whole, get fewer chances than the centers to score. Gretzky scored a record 92 goals in 1981–82 and 87 in 1983–84 with the Edmonton Oilers; Lemieux scored 85 goals in 1988–89 with the Pittsburgh Penguins; and Phil Esposito netted 73 goals with the Boston Bruins in 1970–71.

Because talented centers are a rare breed, they are deeply coveted by NHL teams. Forty-nine centers, the second-largest number of any position, were chosen in the 1997 draft. The only position selected more often was defensemen—94 were chosen—and teams need two of them on the ice at the same time.

"Centers have to recognize where to make the play," says Gary Dornhoefer. "In order for the line to be successful, the center has to know where the wingers are, what they're going to do, and when they'll do it."

"Because centers often develop successful plays with certain wingers," Eric Lindros says, "it's important not to be predictable. You don't want to get into a rut of always doing the same thing. In junior hockey I played with a real talented scorer, Rob Pearson, who had 50 goals one year, and I would always look for him. People would know that I was looking for him. It was the same thing when Adam Oates played with Cam Neely. He'd look for him. The same thing when Oates played with Brett Hull. So you always have to mix up the plays so you didn't become predictable. I was lucky in Philly. I had two guys who I could play with. Mikael Renberg and John LeClair were two quality scorers."

"Forwards have to play close to each other," says Renberg. "You can't play spread out. You have to get traffic in front of the net and crowd the goalie. I'm not a goalie, but it must be pretty easy when all the shots come from the outside. You can see them all."

For his part, Gretzky likes good communication with his wingers. "Communication is the whole game," Gretzky says. "You're always talking, and you're always trying to help each other in the sense of what you'd like to do, what you're comfortable with, and what they're comfortable with. You try to watch it on the video and go over it in practice."

The Greatest Centers

Jean Beliveau

Graceful—and perhaps the best stickhandler in NHL history until Gretzky arrived on the scene—Montreal Canadiens center Jean Beliveau defined the position from the 1952–53 season, when he scored 5 goals in a 3-game callup for Montreal, until his retirement in 1971. So talented as a junior player that Montreal offered him an incredible $105,000 five-year contract, Beliveau won the Hart Trophy as the NHL's most valuable player twice, in 1956 and 1964, and was named an All-Star ten times. Beliveau, one of the league's tallest players at 6-foot-3 (1.9m), was as tough and unselfish as he was talented. Known as a gentleman on and off the ice, Beliveau politely shook hands with opponent Gordie Howe on October 27, 1963, after Howe surpassed Rocket Richard's career goals record. Richard and Beliveau were Montreal teammates. When he retired, Beliveau was the highest-scoring center in NHL history. He had 1,219 points.

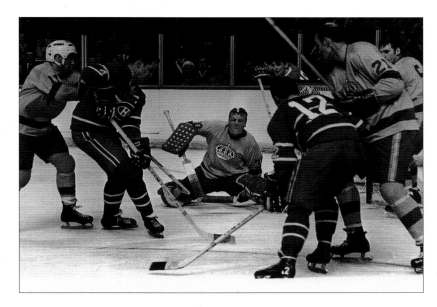

Jean Beliveau was a master at stickhandling in a crowd.

Bobby Clarke

No hockey player past, present, or future could possibly show more heart and determination than Bobby Clarke. A diabetic who wasn't drafted until the Flyers took a chance at number 17 in the 1969 draft, Clarke went on to lead the Flyers to back-to-back Stanley Cups in 1974 and 1975. A grim player who wielded his stick like a sabre, Clarke energized the Flyers as few players could. As the team captain, he shielded rookies from unwanted distractions and cajoled veterans to play better. He was like a coach on the ice. When the Flyers needed a spark, Clarke had the match. Before his Hall of Fame career ended in 1985, Clarke won three Hart Trophies and was ranked fourth on the NHL's all-time assist list. He was a major factor in the Flyers' becoming the first team in modern-day expansion to win the Stanley Cup.

Known for his passion as a player, Bobby Clarke went on to have a successful career as a general manager.

Even after Clarke became general manager of the Florida Panthers in 1993, his playing exploits continued to impress players. "We all admired the way he played on the ice," says John Vanbiesbrouck, a star goaltender for the New York Rangers and the Panthers. "We all wanted to touch part of that, so it could rub off on us and we could say that we were competitors like he was. We all respected the detemination and his opinion on how to be determined."

Phil Esposito

Until scoring goals is no longer the most important thing in hockey, Phil Esposito will rank among the best

centers to have played the game. Sure, Esposito didn't have the all-around game of Clarke or the skill and grace of Beliveau. But he scored 717 goals in his career, making him one of only four players to surpass 700. The older brother of goaltender Tony Esposito, Phil, who played for Chicago, Boston, and New York, was a tough player. Parking himself in the slot like an oak tree, Esposito punched, slapped, and jammed in more goals in a season than anybody until Gretzky joined the league. In 1968 Esposito became the first player to score 100 points in a season, and in 1970–71 he netted 76 goals and amassed 152 points.

Above: Called "Espo" by fans, Phil Esposito went through opponents more often than he went around them.

Howie Morenz

Elected to the Hockey Hall of Fame in 1945, Montreal's Howie Morenz was called the "Babe Ruth of Hockey" and the "Stratford Streak." Small even for those days, the 5-foot-9 (1.8m), 165-pound (74.9kg) Morenz was nonetheless a great shooter. He racked up 40 goals in 44 games during the 1929–30 season—in an era when 40 goals in a season was remarkable—and ended his career with 270 goals. He was the first player to win the Hart Trophy as the NHL's most valu-

Below: Howie Morenz may have been small, but he loved to body-check. He also once broke a goalie's nose with his shot.

able player, and he scored the game-winning goal in 1930 when the Canadiens beat Boston, 4–3, to win their third Stanley Cup (their first at the Montreal Forum). The key to his game was speed and guts. Off the ice, Morenz was a character in the same manner as Babe Ruth—he wore expensive clothes and loved to put on a show for his teammates and friends. Morenz's career came to a tragic end in 1937 when he broke his leg during a game. He died less than two months later when complications from the injury caused his heart to stop. More than 15,000 people attended his memorial service at the Forum.

The Winger

"When the points and goals don't come, you want to contribute in other ways."

KEVIN DINEEN,
Carolina Hurricanes

In baseball, they say, home-run hitters drive Cadillacs while singles hitters drive Fords. It's not exactly the same in hockey, but it's close. The centers are usually the stars of the team. They're the playmakers who set the tone of the game. The wingers, on both the left and right sides, benefit from the center's ability to pass and skate. Of course, that doesn't mean that wingers are less important. They are not. But it's their job to complement the playmaking center by skating along the boards, looking for passes, and skating deep into the corners to fish out loose pucks.

Generally speaking, there are two kinds of wingers: grinders and scorers. The grinders don't score many goals but are relied on to control the puck near the net, set up other players, and play strong defense. Phil Bourque won two Stanley Cups with the Pittsburgh Penguins in such a role. Kevin Dineen, a star scorer with the Hartford Whalers early in his career, became a grinder as his scoring skills diminished.

The scorers, however, take passes from the centers in the circle near the boards or high at the point and rifle shots at the goalies. Wingers Jaromir Jagr, Brett Hull, Brendan Shanahan, and Teemu Salanne have wrist shots that some goalies can barely see. "The bonus comes when there is clutter in the middle," says Shjon Podein, a left winger who, after developing into a defensive star with the Flyers, began to hone his offense. "When you get the puck on the outside you're usually at your highest speed. You usually have a lot of speed playing wing and it adds to the power of your shots."

Because wingers are forced to stay near the boards on defense and protect the lanes, it is important that they can skate backward as well as forward. When the opponent is controlling the puck in the wingers' defensive zone, it's the wingers' responsibility to guard the defensemen at the points and try to intercept passes through the middle of the ice. However, wingers should not be afraid to skate all over the ice if the situation calls for it. "The game has changed a lot," says

Winger Phil Bourque gets one past goaltender Mike Richter.

Theoren Fleury of the Calgary Flames. "The winger's job used to be to go up and down and bang along the boards. It's a little different now. Each guy starts out in that position but it doesn't necessarily mean that over the course of a shift you just go up and down the side that you started on. It's more of a situation now where guys cover up for one another and take other people's position. You can say you're a right winger, but it's more of a flow position."

Gary Dornhoefer, a member of the Philadelphia Flyers' Hall of Fame, says that wingers must know how to play without the puck. "Everybody in the game

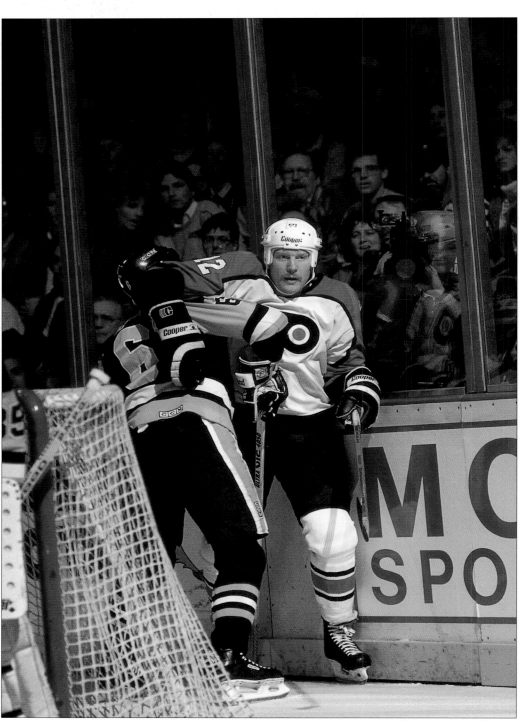

The only way to stop Tim Kerr from scoring goals was to tie him up along the boards, and that wasn't easy. Kerr scored 54 goals or more in four straight seasons during the 1980s.

today can skate," Dornhoefer says. "But there are only a few players who are skilled at getting away from checks and setting themselves up for the shot. Being able to get open makes the center's job that much easier. He doesn't have to stick-handle around looking for an open man. Coaches don't want wingers who don't know how to get open."

Former defenseman Joe Watson knows that wingers who set up camp in the slot caused him the most headaches. John LeClair, who won a Stanley Cup with the Montreal Canadiens, and former Flyer Tim Kerr are considered experts in stationing themselves in front of the goalie and wailing away at the puck. "Those kind of guys challenged you to move them," Watson says, "and they didn't move easily. They'd force you to push them all night. On many nights I'd end up standing next to them instead of moving them."

Even though center is considered the glory position in hockey, hundreds of great wingers have made their way through the NHL. Right winger Mike Gartner of the Toronto Maple Leafs, for instance, scored 30 or more goals for fifteen consecutive seasons. Right winger Mike Bossy of the New York Islanders had nine consecutive seasons in which he scored 50 or more goals. Gordie Howe had twenty-two consecutive seasons in which he scored 20 or more goals. And Boston's Bob Sweeney had 22 game-winning goals, 7 of them coming in overtime.

There have been many great wingers who have patrolled the boards over the years, but few have been braver than left winger Gary Roberts of the Calgary Flames. Sidelined for 89 games midway through the 1995–96 season after undergoing two operations to repair nerve and disk damage to his spine, Roberts returned to the ice in January 1996 and went on to score an incredible 22 goals and 20 assists in just 35 games. Unfortunately for Roberts, he suffered another injury to his neck late in the season and was forced to retire on June 17, 1996. Before he bowed out for good, Roberts was honored with the Bill Masterton Trophy for "perseverance, sportsmanship and dedication to hockey."

Mike Gartner used his blazing speed and accurate wrist shot to score goals.

The Greatest Right Wingers

Mike Bossy

Who knows how many goals Mike Bossy would have scored if his career hadn't been cut short by back problems? Bossy, who won the Calder Cup as rookie of the year in 1978, flashed through the NHL like a glittering comet. He racked up 573 goals playing for those fabulously exciting New York Islanders as they won the Stanley Cup four years in a row, from 1980 to 1983. He had one of the quickest releases of any shooter in the game during his era, and in 1981 he became the first player in thirty-six years to score 50 goals in 50 games. Bossy won the Conn Smythe Trophy as the most valuable player of the playoffs and the Lady Byng Trophy three times.

Bill Torrey, former general manager of the Islanders, says that Bossy's shot was so quick and accurate that it was uncanny. "In his four years of junior hockey he averaged 74 goals per season," says Torrey. "In the NHL it wasn't much less. He had a hard shot, but mostly it was quick. He had a way of appearing out of nowhere. There were games he played in for 58 minutes and you wouldn't see him. You'd say, 'Where the heck is Boss?' Two minutes later, he would score 2 goals and you'd win, 2–1."

Above: Goaltenders would cringe every time Mike Bossy skated into the right circle and raised his stick to shoot.

Guy Lafleur

Many experts call Guy Lafleur the best player of the second half of the 1970s—and with good reason. After having subpar seasons for his first three years in the NHL, Lafleur reeled off six seasons in which he scored no fewer than 100 points and at least 50 goals. Called "the Flower" because that's what his last name means in English, Lafleur led the NHL in scoring for three consecutive seasons and led the Canadiens to four Stanley Cups. He was a star even before he entered the NHL—as a junior player in Quebec he became notorious for his energy and daring moves on the ice. During his professional "major league" career, Lafleur won two Hart Trophies as the league's most valuable player.

Maurice Richard

Maurice "Rocket" Richard was such a popular player in Montreal that the fans there rioted in 1955 when they learned that he had been suspended by NHL president Clarence Campbell for attacking Boston defenseman Hal Laycoe and linesman Clint Thompson in a high-sticking incident.

There have been few clutch scorers in NHL history who have even come close to measuring up to Richard's standard: the Rocket is the only player to have scored 6 playoff goals in overtime, and he has more playoff hat tricks—8—than anyone except Wayne Gretzky, who also has 8. A member of Montreal's famous "Punch Line" (along with Hector "Toe" Blake and Elmer Lach), Richard was the first player to score 50 goals in 50 games and his 543 career goals were an NHL record until Gordie Howe came along. In 1955 Richard, known for his violent temper as well as his scoring touch, scored 5 goals in the final game of the Stanley Cup finals and was named the game's first, second, and third star. Late in his career, Richard played with his younger brother, Henri (known as the "Pocket Rocket"), and Dickie Moore on one of the NHL's most explosive lines. He retired in 1960.

Maurice Richard (center) poses with his brothers, Claude and Henri, whom he played with on the 1959 Canadiens.

Jari Kurri

Kurri, who played his 1,000th NHL game during the 1994–95 season, was a great offensive threat when he teamed with Wayne Gretzky in the glory days of the Edmonton Oilers. When he was traded to the Los Angeles Kings in 1991, Kurri began to concentrate more on his defense. He has great quickness and is an excellent penalty killer. With the Oilers in 1984–85, Kurri set a record for most goals in a season by a right winger, with 71, and became only the third player in NHL history to score 70 or more goals in a season. Brett Hull broke that record with 86 in 1990–91. In 1985–86 Kurri led the NHL with 68 goals and was fourth in scoring with 131 points. In ten seasons with Edmonton, he helped the team win five Stanley Cups.

Jari Kurri knew how to win. Here he poses with the Stanley Cup, which he captured five times while playing with the Edmonton Oilers.

Why was Kurri still playing in 1996 at age thirty-six? "I still have fun," Kurri says. "It's what I like to do. It's as simple as that. That's the bottom line."

The Greatest Left Wingers

Bobby Hull

They called Bobby Hull the "Golden Jet" because of his long flowing locks and his amazing speed on the ice. A powerful skater with shoulders that could unleash the NHL's hardest slapshot at the time, Hull was named to the NHL's first-team All-Star team ten times. His slapshot is reported to have reached the speed of 120 miles (192km) per hour. As a scoring star for the Chicago Blackhawks, he led the league in scoring three times and won the Hart Trophy as the most valuable player twice. "He was a rock," says Philadelphia Flyers left winger Bill Barber. "He had a rocket of a shot. He was flamboyant in how he played, and he was a wide-open kind of player. He had speed and strength, and his personality and attitude matched his talents." Hull, known as one of the NHL's most agreeable personalities, topped Rocket Richard's achievement of 50 goals in a season when he scored 54 in 1965–66.

Bobby Hull is considered by many to be the most complete player ever to play the game.

Mark Messier

A teammate of Wayne Gretzky's in the 1980s with the Edmonton Oilers, Mark Messier took charge of the Oilers after Gretzky was traded to Los Angeles and led the club to its fifth Cup title in seven seasons. Messier won the Hart Trophy as the league's most valuable player and as a winger for Gretzky in Edmonton, Messier is the prototype power forward. Big and powerful with a mean streak, Messier is also a natural leader who commands respect from teammates and opponents alike. Craig MacTavish, a teammate of Messier's on the 1994 Rangers, said he could see in his compatriot's eyes when the big man was preparing to take over a game. In 1994 Messier led the Rangers to their first Cup title in fifty-four years. During the 1995–96 season, he became the twenty-first player in NHL history to record 500 goals. The winner of six Stanley Cup rings, Messier was reunited with Gretzky on the New York Rangers in 1996. In a youth movement by the Rangers, he was traded to the Vancouver Canucks during the 1997-98 season.

Some players score more than Mark Messier. Some play better defense. Nobody is tougher.

Frank Mahovlich

Nicknamed "the Big M," Frank Mahovlich beat out Bobby Hull to win the 1958 Calder Trophy as the NHL's top rookie. A fine skater who could power his way through most defenses, Mahovlich led the Toronto Maple Leafs in scoring from

1960 to 1966 and guided the team to four Stanley Cups. He scored 48 goals in 1960–61 and caused a stir in 1962 when word leaked out at the All-Star Game in Toronto that the Chicago Blackhawks had offered the Maple Leafs $1 million to bring him to their team. One report said that the Hawks had even brought an actual check along with them. Alas, the bait was offered for naught—Mahovlich had already signed with the Maple Leafs.

Ted Lindsay

A member of the great Detroit Red Wings team of the 1950s, Ted Lindsay played on the "Production Line" with center Sid Abel and right winger Gordie Howe. He was the tough guy on the line, taking the pressure off Howe and Abel so they could do all the dirty work along the boards. At the end of the 1949–50 season, Lindsay, Abel, and Howe finished first, second, and third, respectively, in scoring. Thanks in large part to Lindsay's toughness and scoring ability, the Red Wings won seven consecutive regular-season titles and four Stanley Cups in the 1940s and 1950s. He was named to nine All-Star teams, and his 365 goals were the most for a left winger until Bobby Hull set a new standard. When he retired in 1960 after sixteen years in the game—the last three of which he spent with Chicago—Lindsay thought his hockey career was over. After four years out of the game, however, at the age of thirty-nine, he got the urge to play again and rejoined the Red Wings. Lindsay, who said he returned to the ice because he wanted to retire as a Red Wing, lasted only one season after this return. For this single season, however, he scored 14 goals and was among the NHL leaders in penalty minutes.

Bill Barber

Inducted into the Hall of Fame in 1990, Bill Barber, who played with the Flyers for thirteen years, was part of the club's famous "LCB Line," along with Reggie Leach and Bobby Clarke. He is the Flyers' all-time scoring leader with 420 goals; he's second in team history with 883 points and third with 463 assists. Barber played in 6 NHL All-Star Games and was a key member of the Flyers' Cup championship teams in 1974 and 1975. Without Barber complementing the playmaking Clarke, the Flyers probably would not have become the first modern-day expansion team to win the Stanley Cup.

Opposite: Frank Mahovlich, wearing the dark jersey, often used his body to knock opponents off the puck and pass to his teammates in front of the net.

Left: After Bill Barber retired in 1985, he went on to become a successful coach in the American Hockey League.

The Defenseman

"It's not a hard position to play. It's impossible."

JOE WATSON,
former NHL defenseman

playing defense can be the toughest job on a hockey team. While goaltenders may take shots to the face and forwards have to skate more than anyone, defensemen must do it all: they must carry the puck out of their own zone and move it swiftly and accurately up to the forwards. They must know how far to pinch into the offensive zone without leaving their goaltenders vulnerable. They must be able to skate backward as well as the opposing forwards can skate forward. They must be physical and smart, fast and tough. No wonder the job of defenseman is recognized as the position that requires more experience than any in hockey—there is so much to learn about the position that it takes years to pick it all up.

How important are defensemen? In the 1996 draft pick, NHL clubs selected eighty-five defensemen as compared to fifty-four centers and seventy-seven wingers. "The thing about being a defenseman is that most of your mistakes end up in the net," says Joe Watson. "If a forward makes a mistake, it's a turnover. If a goalie makes a mistake, he was left all alone by the defense. If a defenseman makes a mistake, everybody in the rink sees it and knows who to blame."

"You have to be quick in your own end," says Kevin Haller, a defenseman who won the 1993 Stanley Cup with the Montreal Canadiens. "You have to be able to turn the puck over and move it quickly out to the forwards. Being smart is a big part of it. You have to move the puck to the right forward at the right time. If they can get lots of speed going the other way because you gave them a good pass, you'll get plenty of good rushes. Learning when to rush usually comes with experience. Sometimes you think it's a good idea and it isn't. So you've wasted energy because all you did was skate up, turn the puck over and skate hard back. Now you're a little bit more tired for the rest of that shift. As you learn the right times, you can make the most of those opportunities and actually create something. If you just go every time or at the wrong time, you'll eventually end up getting caught up the ice and out of position."

Defensemen regularly run up against several different kinds of rushes from the opponents. They face one-on-one plays, two-on-one plays, and even three-on-one plays. None of them is enjoyable. On one-on-one plays, the defenseman is expected to keep the rushing forward away from the goalie by poke-checking the puck away or by placing his body between the puck and the goalie.

Defensemen are instructed not to bodycheck rushing forwards because a missed check will allow the forward to skate in against an unprotected goalie. However, a defenseman should try to slow down an attacker by leaning his body toward the puck and blocking the lane. Defensemen should remember that because the goalie is relied upon to stop routine shots, allowing such a shot is not bad.

In two-on-one plays, it's the goalie's job to thwart the puck carrier by coming out of the crease and challenging him to shoot. When that happens, the defenseman should cover the trailing forward so that the puck carrier cannot pass to him. Communication and teamwork between the goalie and the defenseman is critical on that play. "Positioning is huge," Haller says. "You have to get to know your partner well, know what he likes to do. Communication is so important."

In the three-on-one, the defenseman has all kinds of problems. The three attackers can pass the puck back and forth whenever they choose and set up all kinds of plays. According to Chris Therien, a member of the 1994 Canadian Olympic team and the 1995 NHL all-rookie team, the best thing for a defenseman to do is to block any passes to the trailing forwards and allow the goalie to take on the puck carrier one-on-one. The forward may beat the goalie and score, but at least the goalie didn't have to slide back and forth trying to protect against three forwards.

"You've got to give your goaltender the best chance you can to make the save," says Therien. "You can't be indecisive. It's almost better to make a mistake than it is to do nothing. At least that way, the goalie knows what he's up against."

"You want to be the best skater you can be, especially backward," says Kevin Haller, who grew up in Trochu, Alberta, where he watched Kevin Lowe and the Edmonton Oilers win five Stanley Cups. "You want to skate as well backward as the forwards can skate forward. If you're a better skater than the guy coming down on you, the advantage is huge. That's the big key. Kevin Lowe was the perfect example for me because every time he got the puck he did something smart. If he had no play, he made the safe play."

Making the safe play is especially important when players such as Wayne Gretzky or Mario Lemieux are careening down the ice toward you. Most defensemen opt to forget everyone else on the ice when the superstar forwards have the puck. The trick, Haller says, is not to be become too aggressive. "If you challenge them too aggressively they'll make you look pretty silly," Haller says. "The best way with most people is to contain them, keep your eye on them, until you're real close and you know there is a one hundred percent chance that you're going to get them. You have to play more conservative when you play against the better players. And a lot of times it can backfire because, with a little more time to operate, those better players can be even better. You have to be real smart."

Experience is the key. "You get to know the forwards," Haller says. "You get to know that Gretzky likes to do certain things with the puck. You get to know that, well, Lemieux can do anything he wants with the puck. It's a constant learning process, and the successful defenseman will constantly keep looking for new things to learn."

It doesn't matter how you play defense as long as you do it well. Kevin Haller uses the crosscheck to his advantage on this play.

There are also some defensemen who play like forwards. Bobby Orr was probably the greatest rushing defenseman of all time. In 1996 Paul Coffey, a vital cog in the Oilers' machine that claimed four Stanley Cups from 1983 to 1988, became the NHL's all-time leader in points among defensemen by carrying the puck all over the ice and setting up his teammates with pinpoint passing. Critics of Coffey's style of play say that he doesn't pay enough attention to the defensive side of the game. But the speedy Coffey, judged by many to be the best skater in the NHL, has won with every team he's played for.

The same can be said of Larry Murphy, who played for Los Angeles, Washington, Minnesota, Pittsburgh, and Toronto during his professional career. Before Murphy became a professional, scouts said that he skated too slowly and didn't shoot the puck hard enough to be a solid defenseman. But Murphy perfected his positional play and took shots only when they presented themselves. By playing to his strengths and avoiding his weaknesses, Murphy became one of the highest-scoring defensemen in NHL history; he will almost certainly wind up in the Hall of Fame.

"If you want to be an offensive defenseman, you have to have that quick first start," says Eric Lindros, who played defense as a youngster before developing into one of the NHL's top centers. "You have to learn when to jump in and when not to. Defensemen of any kind are always playing under pressure. Guys are coming in at you on the forecheck, and you have to make a lot of plays under pressure. In the offensive zone as a forward, if you make a mistake they have to go 150 feet to score. You make a mistake as a defenseman in your own end, they're right on your doorstep. It forces you to think extremely quickly. My father (Carl Lindros) always stressed, when he was involved with my team at the start, that first passes had to be right on the stick, because that gave the other players on the ice time to do something. If the guy has to dig the puck out of his skates or it's not a smooth transition somehow, then you lose that jump when you're going cross ice. You might have had that jump or a two-second hole; now it's screwed up."

Bill Torrey, president of the Florida Panthers, says that few defensemen are accomplished at both ends of the ice. "If you have an airtight defense, it takes a lot of pressure off your goaltending," says Torrey. "I can't recall any Stanley Cup team of any real quality that didn't have an outstanding defense."

Panthers defenseman Ed Jovanovski, a member of the 1996 NHL all-rookie team, says patience is the key. "It's something you've got to be patient with," says Jovanovski of learning the game. "You've got to play your game and get the puck out of your own end. Don't be cute with it. Make the game easy on yourself. Do the simple things because if you get beat, the chances are fifty-fifty that the puck goes in the net."

Retired winger Pat Conacher says that he learned from his years in Edmonton that defense was the key to having a winning team. Since you can't expect to score five goals every game, you have to limit your opponents to two goals or less. Otherwise, Conacher said, you put too much offensive pressure on yourself.

When Edmonton won numerous Stanley Cups in the 1980s and in 1990, they did so with great defense. "We had the most offensive team in the league, but still, the players knew, 'Hey, we can't be giving up shots...if we want to get there,'" Conacher says. "It was one of the focuses of the team, and it didn't just

When someone parks in front of your goal-tender, the only thing you can do is push him back out. Brian Leetch tries to dislodge Dave Reid early in the 1996—97 season.

start in December or January. We started from training camp and worked on that right through until we won the Stanley Cup."

Because of the emphasis on defense, however, there seemed to be a lack of offensive defensemen in the game in the mid-1990s. Phil Housley and Brian Leetch were high scorers, but the likes of Paul Coffey and Raymond Bourque were far and few between. Coffey, the most prolific defensive scorer in NHL history, became a superstar because of his scoring prowess. Some coaches wished he had played better defense, but no one ever complained about his lack of offensive skills. Coffey had 103 points in 1990 with Pittsburgh. For the most part, though, defense was king in the 1990s.

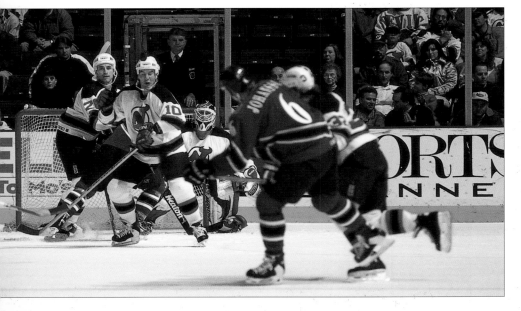

Washington Capitals defenseman Calle Johansson fires a shot from the point as New Jersey Devil Denis Pederson, No. 10, tries to help out in front of goaltender Martin Brodeur.

"In the late eighties, all the kids came up through minor hockey and the minor leagues. Now they've cloned the kids," Conacher says. "They've just cloned too many people. They say to get to the red line and dump it in and bang everything in the other color jersey. Teams are playing that way because it's the only way they can play to win. I think it's taken away all the creative abilities of the players, because if you don't play within that system they're not going to let you play. You don't see guys stickhandle like Denny Savard anymore."

Conacher prefers the system they use in Europe. He says that European coaches let all the players stickhandle the puck and work on their offensive skills. They don't pigeonhole players into positions as quickly as North American coaches. "All this dump-and-chase is bad," Conacher says. "You have to let your defensemen go back, let them handle the puck, let them jump into the play. You never see guys give-and-go anymore. You never see a defenseman come around the net with his wheels going, snap up to the winger, and the winger jump through. That's what's wrong with the game."

Conacher says the NHL became more structured in the early 1990s when the New Jersey Devils and Florida Panthers relied on the defensive trap to slow the game down. The league had featured a free-wheeling attack for much of the 1980s when Wayne Gretzky scored an incredible 215 points in 1985–86 with the Edmonton Oilers.

Then the Devils, under former Canadiens star Jacques Lemaire, won the Stanley Cup over Detroit in 1995 by using a version of the neutral-zone trap. In 1996, the Florida Panthers, under coach Doug MacLean and in front of goalie John Vanbiesbrouck, played their version of the trap all the way to the Cup finals. The trap worked because it took away the passing lanes in the neutral zone and slowed down the offense. It also created a huge controversy. Proponents of aggressive play wanted it outlawed. They said the slow play would kill the game's appeal. But, as Conacher points out, the Devils and Panthers—and practically every other team by 1996—had simply perfected an old system.

"I remember playing against the Canadiens twenty years ago, and they were playing the trap back then," Conacher says. "They pushed everything to the boards and clogged up the neutral zone."

The Greatest Defensemen

Raymond Bourque

If Bobby Orr revolutionized the position of defenseman in Boston, Raymond Bourque perfected it. Big and tough, fast and talented, Bourque became known as an iron man who played more minutes than any player on the ice except the goalies. He is a perennial All-Star selection, having been named to the first team an NHL-record twelve times through the 1996–97 season. Only Gordie Howe, who was also named twelve times, has made as many all-star teams as Bourque.

The best part of Bourque's game is its scope. He is only the second defenseman in NHL history to notch 900 assists, and he led the league in shots in 1994–95. Despite being one of the league's most effective defensemen, Bourque can score like a forward. In 1983 he had 31 goals and 65 assists; three years later, he won the first of his five Norris Trophies as the league's best defenseman. Among defensemen, only Paul Coffey has scored more career points than Bourque. Boston's first pick and the eighth overall in the 1979 draft, Bourque, the Bruins' captain and career assist leader, was the first nongoaltender in NHL history to win both the Calder Trophy as the best rookie and a berth on the first-team All-Star squad.

Although Raymond Bourque is one of the best offensive defensemen in the NHL, his true greatness comes from his willingness to play strong defense, too.

Denis Potvin

Disliked by some in professional hockey for his aggressive arrogance, Denis Potvin was as complete a player as the NHL has ever seen. Chosen first overall in the 1973 draft by the New York Islanders, Potvin won the Calder Trophy as the league's top rookie that year. Continuously improving each season, he scored 101 points in 1979 and went on to help propel the Islanders to four consecutive Stanley Cup championships. A fierce competitor who sometimes injured other players with his jarring checks, Potvin was named the league's best defenseman three times. He was a first-team All-Star five times. When he retired after the 1987–88 season, Potvin was the highest scoring defenseman in the history of the game, with 310 goals, 742 assists, and 1,052 points. His records have since been surpassed by Paul Coffey and Raymond Bourque.

Confidence was never a problem for the flashy Denis Potvin.

"Physically, he was as punishing as anybody," says Bill Torrey. "On the other hand, he could quarterback a power play like nobody else."

Doug Harvey

They called Doug Harvey "Lazy Lightning," not because he didn't produce but because he made the game of hockey seem so easy. A fine athlete who probably could as easily have had careers in professional football or baseball, Harvey was a star for the Montreal Canadiens. Red Kelly won the Norris Trophy as the NHL's best defenseman in 1954, the first year the trophy was awarded. Harvey then won it seven of the next eight years to establish his place among the greatest defensemen in the game. Elegant and shifty, Harvey was famous for his dazzling stick-to-stick passes. He was never one to give in easily to an opponent or even a coach he disagreed with. So Harvey, who won six Stanley Cups with the Canadiens, earned a reputation as a maverick. Elected to the Hall of Fame in 1983, Harvey died of cirrhosis of the liver in 1989.

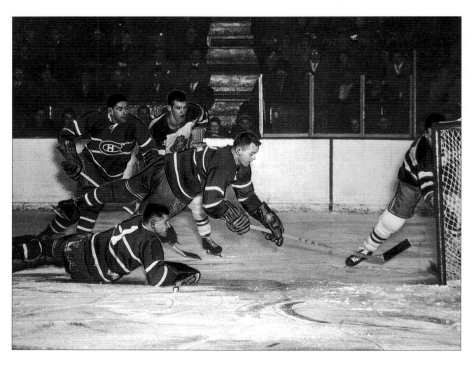

Doug Harvey would often throw his body at the puck in an attempt to block an opponent's shot.

Bill Torrey says that Harvey handled the puck as well as any defenseman who ever played. "He wasn't as nifty a skater as Bobby Orr, but he was an unbelievable puck handler and all around defenseman," says Torrey. "You don't hear that much about him today, but the power play that he was the quarterback on back at the blue line was so good they put in a rule that as soon as a team scores, the guy comes out of the penalty box. He helped define the game as it is today."

Eddie Shore

Although Eddie Shore scored 105 goals in his NHL career, he was considered one of the best defensive players in the league's early years. Perseverance was Shore's middle name. Cut from his college team after a youth spent ranching in Saskatchewan, Shore, an expert at blocking shots by dropping to his knees, made a name for himself in the minor leagues. He was nicknamed the "Edmonton Express" because he was so tough to stop on the rush, something that most defensemen of the era stayed away from. A star for the Boston Bruins, Shore won the Hart Trophy as the NHL's most valuable player four times in the 1930s and was a first-team All-Star seven times.

In 1933 Shore checked Ace Bailey and fractured the great man's skull, resulting in Bailey's premature retirement. The first of three benefit All-Star Games was played in 1934 to honor Bailey, and Shore and Bailey shook hands in a pregame ceremony at center ice.

Known as one of the toughest players in the history of the game, Eddie Shore broke his nose more than a dozen times and needed nearly 1,000 stitches over his fourteen-year career.

Larry Robinson

Larry Robinson played seventeen seasons for the Montreal Canadiens and three for the Los Angeles Kings. Nicknamed "Big Bird" because of his lanky stature, Robinson won five championships in seventeen years with the Canadiens. Through 1995, Robinson was ranked ninth on the all-time list in games played (1,384), third in assists among defensemen (750), and fourth in points among defensemen (958). He also held the overall league records for most career playoff games (227) and most consecutive years in the playoffs (20). He won two Norris Trophies as the best defenseman in the league and a Conn Smythe Trophy as the best player in the playoffs. Robinson is perhaps best known for neutralizing the Philadelphia Flyers' Dave "the Hammer" Schultz in the 1976 Stanley Cup finals. After his playing days ended following his short stint with the Los Angeles Kings, Robinson went on to serve as an assistant coach for the New Jersey Devils and help them win the 1995 Stanley Cup. He became head coach of the Kings in 1995.

The Hockey Hall of Fame

like most other sports, hockey has a Hall of Fame in which it honors its greatest players, coaches, and contributors. Located in downtown Toronto, the Hockey Hall of Fame, which opened in 1961, is a wondrous maze of historic artifacts such as pucks, sticks, and the skates of legendary players; videos; and other memorabilia. The NHL trophies are on display there, and there are video shows and interactive computer terminals.

As with the other halls of fame, the Hockey Hall of Fame has very specific rules. The two basic rules are that players must be retired three years before they are eligible for induction, and only three players per year may be inducted into the Hall of Fame.

However, there have been questions raised over changes in eligibility criteria—because the game has changed so much over the years, players who may have qualified for the Hall in other eras are now being left out. For instance, because of various rule changes in the game itself and simply because offense sells better, more goals are scored in today's game than in the game of the past. Therefore, there are more players with impressive statistics, which sometimes makes the selection process more difficult.

You can't drink out of the Stanley Cup, but you can get pretty close to Lord Stanley's chalice at the Hockey Hall of Fame in Toronto.

To be inducted into the Hall, a player must be nominated and the nomination must be endorsed by at least one of the fifteen members of the induction committee. To determine whether a nominated player is inducted, a secret ballot is called; the player must receive at least 75 percent of the vote to be inducted. If the player receives more than 30 percent of the vote but less than 75 percent, a second ballot is taken.

There are five catagories of induction: players, builders (owners and management), officials, newspaper writers, and radio and television broadcasters. Through the 1996–97 season, there were 209 players, eighty-five builders, thirteen officials and fifty-four media inductees.

There is also a United States Hockey Hall of Fame located in Eveleth, Minnesota. Opened in 1973, there are fifty-four players, nineteen coaches, sixteen administrators, and one referee in the Hall. New members are inducted annually in October and are judged on their contribution to the game in the United States.

The Goaltender

"Once you get to a certain level everything becomes instinct."

RON HEXTALL,
Philadelphia Flyers

h e may wear a mask, but the goaltender is never unknown. A solitary figure in front of the net, the goaltender is the final line of defense against the opponents' forwards. When all else has failed, when the forwards and defensemen are out of position and nowhere to be found, the goaltender is still there. There is nowhere to run for the man in the mask.

"I've been involved in hockey since I was thirteen years old and I have never been able to figure out why anyone puts on the pads," says Brian Burke. "Why anyone would want to face that pressure, I just can't fathom it. I asked Pete Peeters about it once. I said, 'Why do you play, Pete?' He said, 'I'm the only guy on my team who can really determine a game. Of all the players on the ice I'm always the most important one.' And he's right. Someone else might score the winning goal, but unless the goalie plays well that team doesn't win."

In the early days of hockey, goaltenders wore no more clothing or equipment than the other players. The hard shots that goaltenders face in today's game were not yet part of the game. Many shots never even left the surface of the ice, so goalies didn't need masks or other cumbersome equipment. But as the game grew faster and the shots harder, goalies began to add protections. In 1959 Jacques Plante became the first goalie to wear a mask in the NHL, and every other goalie eventually followed suit. Today, a goalie's mask reflects part of his personality or his relationship to the team. John Vanbiesbrouck, the goalie for the Florida Panthers, painted a roaring panther head on his mask. Gerry Cheevers of the old Boston Bruins had stitches etched on his mask in the places where a flying puck would have left scars.

But the mask is not the only equipment that sets the goalie apart from the other players—his gloves are also different. On the hand that holds the stick the goalie wears a special glove called the "blocker." The blocker has a fingered glove on the inside so that the stick can be held firmly in the hand. On the outside, the pad is thick and square to help block shots. The glove on the other hand is known as the "trapper." A wide glove with webbing like a baseball mitt, the trapper is used to catch pucks. With these two gloves, the goaltender can both block and catch shots. Because a goaltender cannot possibly catch or block every shot with his hands, he wears thick padding on his chest and arms. Like the trapper, the chest protector was borrowed directly from a baseball catcher's wardrobe.

To protect his legs, the goalie wears thick leg pads that are quite heavy and warm. Some goalies wear especially light leg pads because they know they will be heavy with sweat at the end of the game. George Merritt of the Winnipeg Victorias was the first goalie to wear leg pads in the Stanley Cup playoffs. He wore cricket pads in an 1896 game against Montreal; the Victorias won, 2–0.

"It's amazing to see all the equipment that goalies have to wear," says coach Scotty Bowman. "And they have to skate well. They have to be smart enough to know the shooters. It's one of the tremendous arts of any sport. To be a goalie and put on all that equipment, most people couldn't even move."

There is more than one technique to stop pucks, and many goalies use more than one style. Some of them, such as Patrick Roy, a three-time Vezina Trophy winner as the NHL's best goalie, use the stand-up style. Roy, who plays for the Colorado Avalanche, stands in the net and challenges the shooters to beat him low to the corners. By staying on his feet, Roy is able to move easily from side to side in the crease and react quickly to shots from all over the ice. Sometimes, when the stand-up doesn't seem workable, Roy uses the butterfly method—he falls to his knees with his skates outward like the wings of a butterfly.

Other goalies, such as the Philadelphia Flyers' Ron Hextall, prefer the flop. When play gets close to the net or a shot is taken, Hextall will flop on the puck and smother it so that no player can steal it. The strategy is successful because, even if he misses the puck and it is regained by his opponents, the lower front of the net is protected by the goalie's prone body. This maneuver can, however, be countered using shots that sail high over the goalie's body.

"Balance on your feet is the most important thing," says Hextall, who won the Vezina Trophy as the league's top goalie and the Conn Smythe Trophy as the

most valuable player of the playoffs in 1987. "A goal-tender has to work on his skating as much as the other players, moving sideways and getting up and down. Lateral movement is very important. People think you just have to stop the puck when it comes straight at you. But when you get in a game the puck comes at you from all over the place."

Above: Usually a butterfly-style goalie, Felix Potvin flops on his side to stop this shot.

Smaller goaltenders who can't cover the net as well as their bigger counterparts and older goalies who can't quite move as quickly as they used to often prefer playing the angles. They move out from the net when the play moves toward them and try to cut down the angle the shooter sees as he approaches. This works well when the shooter is unable to get around the goalie, but if the goaltender allows the shooter to get past him with the puck, it's almost a certain goal.

"You always have to put that last shot, that last game behind you," says Hextall. "When the game before affects the game you're playing, that's when

Harry "Hap" Holmes
was a star in Detroit
in the early days of
pro hockey when no
one wore face masks.
The AHL award for
the team with the
lowest goals-against
average is named
after him.

you're not effective. You can't get overintense because there is a lot on the line. You've got to stay with the same mental preparation that you've used all along. You can't try to jack it to another level or you wind up shooting yourself in the foot. Some guys get scared. Some guys, because of their experience, realize that you have to prepare the same way."

In making saves, the goaltender uses a variety of styles. He can, for instance, kick the puck away in what is called a skate save, or he can make a stick save, knocking it away with his stick. Goalies also stop pucks by stacking their leg pads. That technique requires goalies to lie on their side and place one pad on top of the other to form a wall. Once he stops the puck, the goalie must clear it out of danger. Hextall, who became the first NHL goalie to score a goal on December 8, 1987, is an expert at whizzing the puck out of the defensive zone. But most goalies prefer simply to clear the puck out of the crease by sending it into one of the corners.

Perhaps the toughest play for the goalie is the penalty shot. Awarded to skaters when they are pulled down from behind on a breakaway, the penalty shot pits a single shooter against the goalie. With the other players watching, the skater takes the puck at center ice and skates in alone at the goalie. It's one of the most dramatic one-on-one matchups in sports.

"Once you get to a certain level, everything becomes instinct," says Hextall, who practiced stopping rolled-up sweat socks when he was a youngster. "After you learn the game you're just out there reacting. The moment you start thinking, you're in deep trouble. If you're thinking, you're guessing. What you want to do is anticipate, which is all natural. It just happens."

Dominic Roussel, who has played for Philadelphia and the Winnipeg Jets, adopted a pregame routine that included visualization. Before each game, he would visualize himself making the key save and the tough stop. That way, when he went into the game and was called on to make those plays, he already had an idea of what it took and how it felt to be successful.

Because they are so involved in the games, goaltenders often step up and determine the outcome. Roy and Vanbiesbrouck engaged in a classic goaltending battle in Game Four of the 1996 Stanley Cup finals. The two matched each other save for save until Colorado's Uwe Krupp sneaked a shot past Vanbiesbrouck at 4:31 of the third overtime to give the Cup to the Avalanche.

So what's the toughest part of playing goalie? "Showing up at the rink," says Gerry Cheevers, who won 230 of 418 games in the 1960s and 1970s. "It's the fact that you're the focal point. You're the one with egg on your face all the time. You're the last defense. The pressure is always there."

The Greatest Goaltenders

Ken Dryden

Ken Dryden may not have been the best goalie ever to play in the NHL, but you'd be hard pressed to find one that was more intelligent. After turning down a chance to play at Harvard, Dryden went on to graduate from Cornell and attend law school. Dryden gained attention when he was called up from the minors at the end of the 1970–71 season; he responded by leading the Montreal Canadiens to the Stanley Cup championship. Along the way, he won the Conn Smythe Trophy as the playoffs' most valuable player and the Calder Trophy as the NHL's top rookie. Dryden went on to help his team win six Stanley Cups, four of them consecutive. In seven seasons, Dryden won 258 games and lost only 57. His specialty was the shutout. He had 46 of them, and they helped him earn a 2.24 career goals-against average. After he retired in 1979, Dryden penned a book, *The Game*, which gave readers a fascinating insider's glimpse into the world of hockey and its players.

Shooters had a hard time sneaking shots past Ken Dryden's six-foot four-inch (190cm), 205-pound (92kg) body.

Glenn Hall

Glenn Hall is most famous for his 502 consecutive games at goal for the Detroit Red Wings and Chicago Blackhawks from 1956 to 1963. A seven-time first-team All-Star and four-time second teamer, Hall played in each of the 70 games in his rookie year and won the 1956 Calder Trophy as rookie of the year. From that point on, Hall was the NHL's ironman. He played in an era before goalies wore masks, so his streak of 33,135 consecutive minutes is even more remarkable. Hall even played one game in the 1957 semifinals against Boston despite needing twenty-five stitches after taking a shot to the face. Hall led the Blackhawks to the Stanley Cup championship in 1961 and the St. Louis Blues to the finals in 1967. He also won the Conn Smythe Trophy that season as the most valuable player of the playoffs.

Glenn Hall frustrates Dave Keon in this dramatic one-on-one encounter.

Terry Sawchuk

Terry Sawchuk played for Detroit before Hall joined the Red Wings. Hampered by injuries and personal problems throughout his life, Sawchuk nevertheless won the Calder Trophy as the league's best rookie in 1951. From there, his career took off. He won the Vezina Trophy as the goaltender with the best goals-against average in 1952, 1953, and 1955, and he ended his career with 103 shutouts, the most of any goalie in NHL history. Sawchuk had 11 shutouts as a rookie and 4 in the 1952 playoffs to lead the Wings to the Cup championship. Ever an innovator, Sawchuk was credited with inventing the crouch that nearly every goalie uses these days to see through the tangle of players who routinely gather in front of goalies.

Terry Sawchuk used both his leg and stick to protect the net against the Montreal Canadiens.

Patrick Roy

Patrick Roy showed just how valuable he can be when he helped turn the Colorado Avalanche, perennial runners-up as the Quebec Nordiques, into Stanley Cup champions in 1996. After being traded from Montreal to Colorado early in the season, Roy went on to help his team win 22 more games and eventually led the Avalanche to the title. A big goalie who is most vulnerable between his skates, Roy led all goalies in minutes played in 1994–95. He won the Conn Smythe Trophy as the most valuable player of the playoffs in 1986 and 1993 and the Vezina Trophy as the best goaltender in 1989, 1990, and 1992. Through 1997, Roy had played in 7 NHL All-Star Games and finished with the league's lowest goals-against average four times.

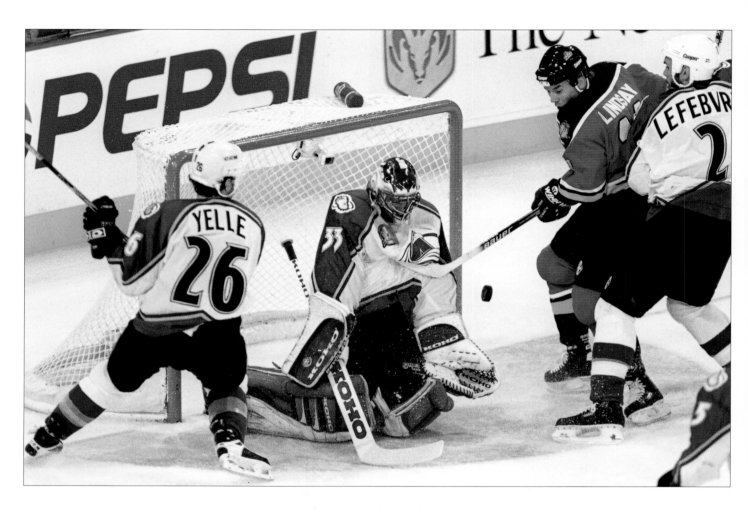

Above: Patrick Roy used his trademark butterfly technique to win four straight games over Florida in the 1996 Stanley Cup finals.

Right: This injury required seven stitches and led Jacques Plante to become the first goalie to wear a face mask in an NHL game.

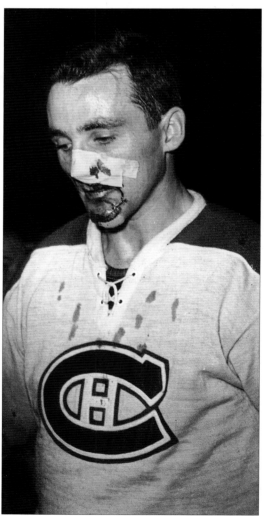

Jacques Plante

The goalie for the great Montreal Canadiens of the late 1950s, Jacques Plante introduced roving goalies and face masks to the NHL. An excellent skater and stickhandler, Plante would often go into the corners to fish out pucks and aid his defensemen. Years later, Flyers goalie Ron Hextall would copy Plante's style with great success. On November 1, 1959, Plante, after having been cut earlier in the game on a shot by the Rangers' Andy Bathgate, donned a primitive face mask. The practice caught on, and goalies have worn masks ever since. Plante may have been an unpopular player in Montreal (he was a loner who some fans claimed used his injuries as an excuse for poor play), but he found fame in St. Louis. Coming out of retirement in 1969, Plante teamed with Glenn Hall and won the Vezina Trophy.

The Tough Guys

hockey tough guys have been labeled "enforcers" and "goons" by fans and the media, but the players whom they protect, the Wayne Gretzkys and Mario Lemieuxs of the world, would hate life without them.

Usually big and strong with a mean streak to boot, the tough guys go after opponents who have wronged their team in some way. If a player high-sticks a top scorer and cross-checks a key defenseman, the tough guy will hunt that player down and get even. When Montreal defenseman Chris Chelios clobbered Philadelphia's Brian Propp in the playoffs one year, Flyers goalie Ron Hextall, one of the most fiery goalies ever to play the game, chased down Chelios, attacked him, and got suspended for the beginning of the next season.

"The sign of a good fighter is that he's not afraid to get hit," says Gary Dornhoefer, who played alongside Dave "the Hammer" Schultz for the Flyers in the 1970s. "You want guys who aren't afraid to take three shots to the chin to get in one real good shot himself. Those guys have to have no fear. They have to be willing to fight anyone, and the good ones always will."

Behn Wilson of the Flyers was one of the toughest fighters of the 1970s, when the Flyers were known as the "Broad Street Bullies." Clark Gillies was feared as a fighter in his day, too. Gillies, a first-round draft pick of the New York Islanders in 1974, was a talented player. He played in the 1978 All-Star Game and scored a combined 319 goals for the Islanders and Buffalo Sabres. But he knew how to throw his fists, too. "He didn't fight that much, but when he did he won," says Gary Dornhoefer.

John Ferguson was the muscle behind the Canadiens in their championship seasons of 1965, 1966, 1968, and 1969. Before the burly Ferguson arrived on the scene, the talented-but-small Canadiens couldn't do much in the playoffs. Once Ferguson joined the team, the smaller playmakers on the team felt safe. "He was a fierce guy who would get this look in his eye," says Joe Watson. "Then, look out."

Gordie Howe was one of the toughest players, too, when he wasn't scoring goals. "Gordie could be really mean," says Joe Watson. "He had those long slop-

Being tough is risky. Gordie Howe missed a check in the 1950 NHL playoffs, smashed headfirst into the boards and wound up in the hospital.

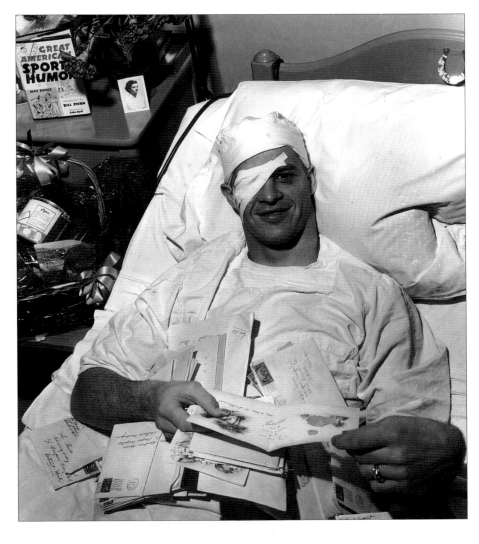

ing shoulders, and he wasn't afraid to use his stick. One night in 1957 he and Louie Fontinato got into a fight, and Gordie carved his ear off. I remember looking at a picture of the fight and Lou was lying there against the boards and his ear was just hanging there like it was ready to drop right off."

For sheer wildness, few players matched Dave "Tiger" Williams and Dave "the Hammer" Schultz. Both men fought often and with gusto. But neither would be classified as a pugilistic talent. Dale Hunter and Marty McSorley, two modern-day fighters, are both much sought after for their toughness. Esa Tikkanen was nicknamed "the Grate One" for his ability to irritate opponents, and Claude Lemieux, in addition to winning back-to-back Stanley Cups with New Jersey in 1995 and Colorado in 1996, has made a living from driving his opponents to distraction.

Many people, including Wayne Gretzky, do not like fighting in the game, however, and there have been many pushes to end it. The NHL thought it had solved the fighting problem in 1959 when a rule was instituted that prevented players from leaving the bench to join fights. Not so. In 1971, the league ruled that the third player already on the ice who entered a fight would be automatically booted out of the game. And in 1976, it was ruled that players who started fights would be booted out of the game with a game misconduct penalty.

None of this, however, has stopped the fighting, especially when referees often allow fighters to escape with nothing more than a minor penalty. As of the end of the 1995–96 season, the NHL had determined that fans liked the fighting as long as the game does not suffer.

Above: It's not easy to throw punches while standing on skates. Most hockey fights are more shoving and grabbing than anything else.

Opposite: Tempers often erupt, and tough guys, like Lyle Odelein (left) and Mathieu Schneider, wind up taking out their frustations on each other.

The Coach

"You can't demand respect. You have to earn it."

TERRY MURRAY,
Philadelphia Flyers coach

I t's not easy being a coach in the modern era of hockey. Players are paid millions of dollars a year to draw fans to the rink. Wayne Gretzky signed a contract with the New York Rangers in 1996 that paid him $5 million for one season. Most coaches earn much less than many players, though a good coach is essential to a team's success. Coaches must earn the respect of all the players. Every player must believe in the coach's systems and strategy for the team to be successful. "You have to have a relationship with your players so that when you walk into the dressing room in the morning and say 'Good morning' there are going to be players who say 'Good morning' back to you," says coach Terry Murray.

For most coaches below the NHL level, teaching the fundamentals of the game takes up most of their time. "(A player has) to learn how to skate, to shoot, to pass," says Murray, who coached the NHL's Washington Capitals and Philadelphia Flyers. "You've got to know the real fundamentals of reading the game as it's being played. If you have a solid foundation, whether you're a junior player, a minor-league pro, or in the NHL, over the long haul of the season, you have to have a base to be successful." When Murray took over the Flyers coaching job from Terry Simpson in 1994, his first task was to teach the players how to play better defense. Murray believes that defense wins most hockey games. Nearly every club has a star scorer, a player no opposing team can keep from scoring goals for very long. That being the case, many coaches believe that teams who perfect their defensive games eventually win more games. Scoring goals involves more luck than playing solid defense does. "You can be an exciting team, a run-and-gun team, an explosive team on the offensive part of the game. But if you're going to play pursue-the-puck style on a consistent basis, you're going to pay the price," Murray says. "If you learn how to play the game defensively, that will be rewarded with some championships down the road."

Of course, it is just those championships that every coach is aiming for. While the old cliché of "taking one game at a time" certainly holds true, a smart coach will inspire his players by giving them something to strive for. "You have to prepare yourself in training camp to know that your goal is to win the Stanley Cup," Murray said. "When you begin with the end in mind, there is a very clear direction of where you want to get to. Then you talk about the commitments and the sacrifices and the style that you're going to have to play throughout the year, the long haul of the season. You have to map out your strategies and your practices. Let the players clearly know what the overall plan is."

Bill Barber, who went from playing to scouting to coaching in the minor leagues, says that for him the hardest part of coaching is dealing with players who

In seven seasons of coaching at Washington and Philadelphia, Terry Murray has never missed the playoffs through 1997.

don't go all out to win. "I have a hard time digesting how you lose," Barber said. "The little mistakes that are made, I can live with them. But when the effort isn't there and the heart isn't there, that's where it's tough. I like to see the guys have fun, but fun is winning. There are games that we've lost but that I felt comfortable with, and I was proud of the guys. But there are also games that I left very frustrated. I was in shock at times."

Not all coaches are serious-minded all the time. Roger Neilson used to take his dog on the ice with him at practice when he coached the New York Rangers.

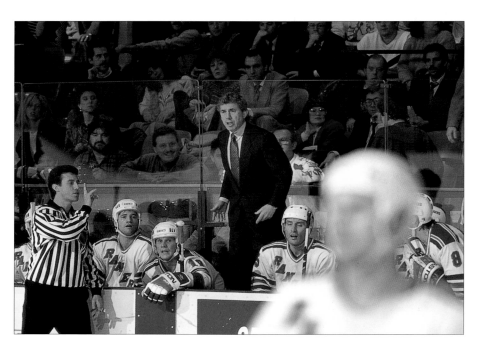

Roger Neilson often expressed his disagreement with the officials by standing on the bench and shouting loudly.

He also took a trip to New Zealand in 1993 and dove off a two-hundred-foot (60m) cliff with a bungee cord tied to his ankle. He's also called "Captain Video" because of his love of using video tapes as teaching tools. Terry Crisp would skip morning warmups altogether on game days with the Tampa Bay Lightning and sit in the coaches' room telling funny stories. Fred Shero was called "the Fog" when he coached the Flyers because of the vacant look that masked his ingenious mind.

"We never really knew what Freddie was saying most of the time," says Joe Watson of Shero. "He'd go on and on about something and we'd all sit there and look at each other with these looks on our faces. Then, a week or two later, you'd be lying in bed and it would come to you. That's what he meant. And it made sense then."

"Freddie didn't seem to have the ability to talk to people one-on-one," says Gary Dornhoefer. "He could talk to a group and be very articulate and comfortable. But he seemed terrified to talk to people one-on-one. I don't think I ever dealt with him in my entire career one-on-one. He'd always call in the line or the forwards or the veterans to speak to. But he never dealt with people one-on-one."

Larry Robinson, coach of the Los Angeles Kings, was a great example of a hardworking player in his twenty years in the league with Montreal and Los Angeles, and he depends on that experience to communicate with his players. "I don't think you pass on your knowledge," says Robinson. "It's an ongoing process where you try to help the younger players, and even the older players, through your own experiences. Knowledge is something that you have to get yourself. The problem that some coaches have is that they try to change the players into something that they're not. I think our job should be to mold the talents that they have and try to make them better players. You look for their weaknesses and try to make them better in different areas."

Robinson was challenged in 1996–97. His Los Angeles Kings team was full of young players who really didn't know each other very well. "It took a lot of patience to run that team," says Robinson. "That was the key. Young guys are going to make mistakes. But we knew if we could live through our mistakes and survive through our mistakes and get better each day, we'd be all right. We had something that we hadn't had in the history of our organization and that was depth in most areas, and that impressed me the most."

No matter what their personalities, coaches share at least one thing: the desire for success. And success requires several things: "Stay healthy. Get lucky. Everybody have a career year," Murray says. "Then you can have some good results."

The Greatest Coaches

Scotty Bowman

Scotty Bowman does not look like a hockey coach. Short and stocky, he sometimes looks a bit awkward on skates. But no coach in the history of the NHL has been responsible for more victories than William Scott Bowman. Through 1997 the Montreal native had coached for St. Louis, Montreal, Buffalo, Pittsburgh, and Detroit and won a league-record 1,013 games. He had lost just 460 games, resulting in a league-record .659 winning percentage. Bowman also had a league-record 178 playoff victories and seven Stanley Cup championships, including the 1997 title, to his credit. Only Toe Blake has more championship rings. Elected to the Hockey Hall of Fame in the builder category, Bowman led the Canadiens to five championships in eight seasons. He is the only coach to guide four different teams—Montreal, Pittsburgh, Detroit, and Buffalo—to the finals, and he's also worked as a general manager and director of player personnel.

"I've been fortunate," says Bowman, who completed the 1996–97 season with more than 1,000 career victories. "I kept coaching because I wanted to try and win 1,000 games. It seemed like it was impossible. Now when I'm 25 games away, I keep motivated that way. When I broke in with St. Louis we had a tremendous goalie in Glenn Hall. When I got to Montreal I had Kenny Dryden. Certainly Guy Lafleur and Mario Lemieux are among the best ever to play, and I got to work with them. The toughest part of coaching is when you don't have a very talented team, and you've got to mold it into one. It's even tough to mold a great team, getting the players not to be jealous of each other and play as a team. The team goals have to be the number one focus point."

Brian Burke, the NHL's director of hockey operations, says that Bowman's personality is as impressive as his hockey resume. "Scotty is an incredibly bright guy," says Burke. "His insights on the game are amazing. I still love to sit and talk hockey with Scotty. You learn so much. So start off with a great brain, a great hockey mind. Then couple it with the fact that he's a good guy, a nice man. He's easy to be around, but he's also very intense. People say he's as good a bench coach in

Scotty Bowman's (right) aloofness sometimes irked his players, but no one can argue with his success.

the modern era as there ever was as far as the matchups he gets on the ice. He also motivates players well, and that's not easy to do in the nineties."

Bowman says that his favorite memories are of the great players he worked with. "You don't do a lot of coaching with them, but you look back and see how good those players really were," says Bowman, who only had to point his stars in the right direction. "You don't notice it when you're coaching them and you're with them, but you do when you look back. You see how great they really were."

Hector "Toe" Blake

A member of the Montreal Canadiens' famous "Punch Line" (along with Rocket Richard and Elmer Lach), Toe Blake, nicknamed the "Old Lamplighter," was a

Toe Blake owned an 82-37 playoff record with the Canadiens.

great player in the 1940s with Montreal. When he retired as a player and became the Canadiens' coach, Blake led the club to eight championships from 1955 to 1968. Blake's Montreal teams had no equals. Under Blake, the Canadiens became the first team ever to win the Stanley Cup five seasons in a row. He turned the team into such a dominating unit on the power play that the NHL voted in 1956 to allow penalized players to rejoin the game after one goal was scored on the power play. Up to that point, penalized players had served out their entire time in the penalty box. Using his experiences as a player as his guide, Blake was able to blend the talents of unproven youngsters and grizzled veterans into a Montreal dynasty. One of his craftiest coaching moves was to have winger Gilles Tremblay shadow Gordie Howe all over the ice in 1963 when Howe was trying to score a goal and tie Rocket Richard's record for goals in a career. The plan didn't work and Howe scored anyway, but it was a good idea.

Glen Sather

They call him "Slats" with deep respect. Few coaches in NHL history have had more success in such a short span as former Edmonton Oilers coach Glen Sather. A twenty-year veteran of the Oilers organization in 1996, Sather served as the coach and general manager of the Oilers for their first ten seasons in the NHL, stepping down in 1989. In winning five championships with the Oilers in the 1980s, Sather racked up a .706 winning percentage in the playoffs, the best in NHL history. Sather was best known for his ability to get individuals to play together as a team. Between 1982 and 1988, Sather led the Oilers to five Stanley Cup finals, winning four of them (1984, 1985, 1987, and 1988). In 1986 he won the Jack Adams Award as the NHL's coach of the year. Sather ended his coaching career with a record of 442–341–99. After he stepped down as coach and assumed the mantle of general manager, Sather helped the Oilers win the 1990 championship. He also coached Team Canada in the 1996 World Cup.

Fred Shero

Fred Shero was perhaps the most innovative coach ever to set foot in a hockey rink. Freddie the Fog got his nickname because his mind and his body never seemed to be in the same place at the same time. However, he could, and often would, talk hockey for hours on end. Before he left the Flyers in 1978 to coach the New York Rangers, Shero directed the Flyers to back-to-back Stanley Cups in 1974 and 1975. He is credited with hiring the first assistant coach and instituting morning skates on gamedays. Shero is perhaps best known for his inspiring speeches. Before the Flyers won their second Stanley Cup, Shero told his players, "Win tonight and we will walk together forever." They did and they have.

Fred Shero knew how to win. He won 390 games in ten NHL seasons.

Al Arbour

Only Scotty Bowman has more career victories, more playoff games coached, and more playoff victories than Al Arbour. Teamed with general manager Bill Torrey, Arbour coached the New York Islanders to four consecutive Stanley Cup championships from 1980 to 1983. Through the 1995–96 season, Arbour was the NHL's all-time leader in games coached, with 1,606. In 1992 Arbour, who won Stanley Cup rings as a player in 1954, 1961, and 1964, won the Lester Patrick Award for outstanding service to hockey in the United States. A resilient coach who couldn't refuse a challenge, Arbour returned to the Islanders bench in 1988 after stepping down in 1986 to serve as the club's vice president of player development.

"Al, being one of the great defensive defensemen, was the guy I wanted when I needed a coach for the Islanders," says Bill Torrey, former general manager of the Islanders. "I saw him when he was an assistant coach in St. Louis. I also knew him in Rochester when he worked with Punch Imlach and the Leafs were winning their Cups. There was no doubt in my mind that of the available coaches he would be the best guy. I was right. What, in my mind, made him not only a good coach but a cut above was that once we got our defensive game down, once the defense was in, we started bringing in offensive players. And Al had the ability to change from just being a defensive guy to taking advantage of the offensive skills that our scouting staff had added."

The General
Manager

"You grow to like your players.
You grow to admire them.
But trading them is often your job."

BRIAN BURKE,
former general manager of the Hartford Whalers

every organization has to have an ultimate boss, and for a hockey team that boss is the general manager. The owner may pay the bills, and the coach may call the shots on the ice, but the general manager is the man who puts the team together. Using trades to acquire players, money to sign free agents, and instinct in plucking players in the entry draft, the general manager builds and rebuilds year after year. It's his job to determine his team's needs after each season and fill them for the coming season.

Eric Lindros, who was acquired by the Flyers in a monster trade with Quebec in 1992, likens the job of a general manager to that of a card player. "It's like trying to make a gin hand," Lindros says. "If you take in one card you've got to throw out another."

To acquire Lindros, Flyers general manager Russ Farwell and club president Jay Snider made the biggest trade in the history of the league. They sent six players, two number one draft picks, and $15 million to the Quebec Nordiques. Before that time, the 1988 trade that sent Wayne Gretzky, Mike Krushelnyski, and Marty McSorley from Edmonton to Los Angeles for two players, three number one draft picks, and $15 million had been the biggest.

Like many players and coaches, general managers can be a colorful lot. Harry Sinden is a cantankerous, outspoken hockey man who built a playoff dynasty in Boston. After making it to the 1996 playoffs, the Bruins had qualified for post-season play twenty-nine years in a row, the longest streak in professional sports. "Harry knew the game as well as anybody in the NHL at the time—still does," says Joe Watson, who broke in with Sinden in 1964. "He understood the players even though he was a son of a bitch with them. He also knew the town he worked in. Boston didn't want to spend a lot of money for players back then, so Harry had to do a lot with a little. I really respect the job he's done."

Keith Allen, the general manager of the Flyers from 1970 to 1983, was called "Keith the Thief" for the great trades he engineered. When Allen traded for Reggie Leach from California, the NHL stepped in and forced Allen to redo the deal so that it wasn't so one-sided. "Keith was a great general manager not only because of his trades but because he was so classy," says Gary Dornhoefer. "You could talk to him one-on-one and get the impression that he really cared, that he was listening. You don't get that with a lot of guys."

Times have changed, however, and many general managers are more cautious than their counterparts of the past. "The money has changed it," says Bill Torrey.

"A general manager could make a mistake before and regret it. But today you could be making a million-dollar mistake. The financial pressure now is huge. Going back years ago, you'd spend sixty percent of your time evaluating the talent of the players, nothing else. Now it's almost the reverse. You can't make talent decisions without having a financial decision first. Not that there is anything wrong with that. . . ."

For Brian Burke, who served as general manager at Hartford and assistant general manager to Vancouver's Pat Quinn, trading players is the hardest part of the job. "You grow attached to them," says Burke. "I remember when we traded Richie Sutter from Vancouver to St. Louis, and he just sobbed. When we told him he had been traded he left the room sobbing. I remember that Pat Quinn looked about a hundred years old. He said to me, 'I can't believe I just traded this guy when we're trying to find twenty more guys with his commitment and intensity.'"

Burke also notes that critics are everywhere. "It's a job where every single move you make is instantly scrutinized closely and either applauded or criticized," says Burke. "You're out there alone. Even if your staff says, 'Make the trade, make the trade.' They might be unanimous on the trade. But the guy who gets blamed if the trade doesn't work out is you. Every draft pick, every trade, every coach you hire, every single thing is instantly scrutinized by the media and the fans. So you have to like that pressure. You have to thrive on that pressure."

Scotty Bowman, who served as coach and general manager for Buffalo and as coach and director of player personnel for the Detroit Red Wings, says that working both jobs simultaneously had its drawbacks. "There's advantages but there's also some disadvantages," says Bowman. "You probably don't do as much managing as you should. Coaching is probably your first love. You do the managing, but when you have to divide your time you sort of spend more time coaching. Managing is a lot of being on the phone, and that's very time-consuming."

Still, building a team can be a very rewarding experience. "One of the most memorable things for me was when we managed to get Pavel Bure out of his contract with the Soviet Red Army team and into the NHL," says Brian Burke. "It was a very gruelling and emotionally exhausting process but well worth it. He's an exceptional hockey player, and that was one event that I was very drained by but very proud of. The result was excellent."

Former Canucks assistant general manager Brian Burke gives some on-ice advice during a Canucks practice.

The Greatest General Managers

Lester Patrick

A star player for the Montreal Wanderers and the Renfrew Millionaires in the early days of the game, Patrick went on to achieve great things as a coach and general manager. He helped organize the Pacific Coast Association and joined the New York Rangers in 1926 as coach. For the 1932–33 season, Patrick took over as general manager of the Rangers and directed the team to its second Stanley Cup. He coached the Rangers to their first Stanley Cup in 1927–28 and served as general manager of the Rangers through the 1945–46 season and won another Cup in 1939–40. During his sixteen years with the Rangers, they failed to miss the playoffs only once. Patrick was elected to the Hockey Hall of Fame in 1947, and soon thereafter a trophy for outstanding service to hockey in the United States was named after him.

Above: Harry Sinden has served as coach, general manager, and president of the Boston Bruins.

Right: Serge Savard was responsible for picking goalie Patrick Roy in the third round of the 1984 draft.

Harry Sinden

Harry Sinden began his twenty-fifth season as general manager of the Boston Bruins in 1996, and his success proves that general managers don't need NHL experience to build teams. Sinden never played even one NHL game—he honed his coaching skills in the minor leagues—but the longtime coach and general manager directed the 1968 Bruins to their first playoff appearance in nine years and the 1970 Bruins to their first Stanley Cup championship in nearly thirty years. Bruins teams directed by Sinden won six conference titles and 10 division championships. None of Sinden's teams have had losing records, and the Bruins' streak of twenty-nine consecutive seasons in the playoffs is the most of any professional team in any sport. Sinden also put together the team of NHL players that beat the Soviets in the 1972 Summit Series, 4 games to 3. Sinden was enshrined in the Hockey Hall of Fame's builder category in 1983.

Serge Savard

Until he was fired in 1995, Montreal general manager Serge Savard ran one of the most successful clubs in hockey. Elected to the Hockey Hall of Fame in 1986, Savard was named general manager of the Canadiens in 1983. He then directed the team to 2 championships, three conference

crowns, four division titles, and playoff appearances in eleven of twelve seasons. As a defenseman, Savard played sixteen seasons, won 8 championships with Montreal, and in 1969 became the first defenseman to win the Conn Smythe Trophy as the playoffs' most valuable player. As the Canadiens' general manager, he directed the club to Cup titles in 1986 and 1993.

Keith Allen

Former Flyers general manager Keith Allen cut his hockey teeth by winning the Stanley Cup with the 1954 Detroit Red Wings, so it was no surprise when, as

general manager, he led the Flyers to back-to-back Cup championships in 1974 and 1975. The 1988 winner of the Lester Patrick Trophy for outstanding service to hockey in the United States, Allen served as general manager of the Flyers from 1969 to 1983. In addition to winning two Stanley Cup rings, Allen took four teams to the finals and ended his career with a 563–322–194 record. Nicknamed "Keith the Thief" for his trading prowess, he acquired Rick MacLeish, Reggie Leach, Bernie Parent, and Mark Howe through trades. He also drafted Bill Barber, Ron Hextall, Brian Propp,

Keith Allen became an executive vice president with the Flyers after retiring as general manager.

and Pelle Lindbergh. Allen was inducted into the Hall of Fame builder category in 1992.

Bill Torrey

Bill Torrey's management career would have ranked him with the best general managers in the history of the game had he ended it in 1993 when he left the New York Islanders. But Torrey's career didn't end there. He went to the expansion Florida Panthers as team president and helped build a team that lost to the Colorado Avalanche in the 1996 Stanley Cup finals. As general manager of the

Islanders from 1972 to 1992, Torrey, infamous for his collection of bow ties, built a team that won four consecutive Stanley Cups from 1980 to 1983. Among the players Torrey drafted for the Islanders were Mike Bossy and Denis Potvin. One of his most famous trades came in 1980 when he dealt Billy Harris and David Lewis to the Los Angeles Kings for Butch Goring. One of the game's best all-around centers at the time, Goring went on to win the

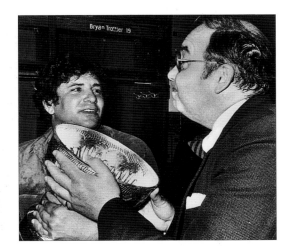

Bill Torrey was the first person hired by the expansion Islanders in 1972.

Conn Smythe Trophy in 1981 as the most valuable player of the playoffs.

The Traveling Secretary

With the heavy travel schedule that hockey teams face today, even amateur and minor league teams need people to schedule buses, hotels, flights, and meals for the team on the go. These people, known today under a number of titles, are basically the traveling secretaries. NHL travel coordinators must handle forty-two road trips per season and additional preseason and postseason journeys. They're responsible for economical, safe, punctual travel, but if you have ever planned even the simplest trip, you know how easily things can go wrong. Imagine planning such a trip not for you and a friend or two, but for twenty-five players, three coaches, two trainers, four broadcasters, and a truck full of equipment. Many things often go wrong. Joe Kadlec, the director of team services for the NHL's Philadelphia Flyers since the team's inception in 1967, has plenty of old war stories.

"It was in the 1960s, and one time we had a snowstorm in Montreal," says Kadlec. "The Canadiens and the Flyers had to go together on a train to Toronto. The Flyers were going to fly back to Philly, and the Canadiens were going onto another train. So we ordered a car for ourselves, and the Canadiens get on their car, and we get on ours. Suddenly, we see the Canadiens eating, and we ordered food. So we think, 'They've got our food.'

"So we go up to some of the Canadiens, and they say, 'You want this sandwich? Take this sandwich.' They (the sandwiches) were awful. A bit later, here comes this porter, and he says, 'We've got your food. It's up in the club car.' So we got it straightened out. But the Canadiens were willing to give us their food, as long as it was crappy."

The Scouts

"Today's game is so fine-line
that an error in judgment,
as far as an evaluation of a player,
can be very costly to your team."

BILL BARBER,
former director of scouting for the Philadelphia Flyers

Some people consider playing goaltender the roughest job in hockey, and they have a point. Facing one-hundred-mile-per-hour (160kph) slapshots can't be fun, no matter what those wacky goalies say. But most goalies are paid very well and spend their time on the road in first-class hotels and restaurants. That's not the case with scouts, who really have the roughest job in the game.

Scouts are the people who search the world for the best players. In baseball, they're called "bird dogs" because they "beat the bushes," looking, not for the bird brought down by the hunter but for the player, preferably the one that no other scout has spotted, who could benefit their team the most. They are the eyes and ears of the team they work for. Pro scouts evaluate the players on other pro teams in case their general manager needs to make a trade. Amateur scouts search the junior leagues and colleges of North America and the hockey rinks of Europe for the young stars of tomorrow who are still developing today.

The hours the scouts work are long, and their task is demanding. Scouts must keep detailed evaluations of the players they watch. Does he shoot the puck hard? Can he skate well? Is he coachable? There are many facets they must examine to determine whether a player is a good fit for their team. Is he happy with the team he is playing for now? Is his team willing to trade him? Can he adapt to life in this city? It's the scout's job to weave all this information into an organized assessment and give his general manager a detailed analysis of the player's worth.

Many scouts are former players who still love to work around the game. Their knowledge of the game and the leagues they wander through is an invaluable tool. Some are simply hockey enthusiasts who have studied the game and, like the former players, love its drama and tradition. Despite their differences, all scouts have one thing in common: they work very hard.

"You don't want to have too young of a family," says Bill Barber, who served for seven years as director of pro scouting for the Flyers, one of the first teams to devote someone full-time to scouting other pro teams. "The travel is very hectic to stay on top of the players. Especially at the pro scouting level, where you have twenty-six NHL teams. You have eighteen American League teams. You have twenty or so International Hockey League teams. You end up covering about fifty, sixty teams on your circuit. So, you run around to about 24 games a month. Your time at home is minimal."

Barber was lucky to work for the Flyers. Based in Philadelphia, he could drive to Washington, New Jersey, and New York to catch games. His children were old enough so that they didn't miss him as much as younger children might

have. Scouts in the far west aren't so lucky when it comes to travel. Both pro and amateur scouts are forced to drive long distances through the prairies of western Canada and the United States to attend games. Russ Farwell, former Flyers general manager and a highly successful general manager in the Western Hockey League, says that flying small planes to remote outposts in nasty weather to scout a prospect in a junior league is commonplace—and few of those plane rides are smooth.

"It's very demanding," Bill Barber says. "There's not much written about it. It's a very behind-the-scenes thing. But it's very valuable because of the trades that teams make and obviously because of the draft. You have to have the right read on the right players. When your boss, the general manager, asks you for an opinion, you have to be accurate with it."

Barber and Bob Clarke, the general manager of the Flyers, did a nice job of working together in 1995 when they acquired defenseman Karl Dykhuis from the Chicago Blackhawks. The Hawks' first-round pick in the 1990 draft, Dykhuis got buried behind the other defensemen in the Blackhawks organization and languished for three seasons in the minor leagues with the Indianapolis Ice. Clarke had seen Dykhuis play before, though, and he sent Barber out to scout him. Barber reported that Dykhuis was still a solid player, so Clarke sent career minor-leaguer Bob Wilkie to the Hawks in exchange for Dykhuis. Dykhuis made the Flyers after just one game in the minors and went on to become a key performer on the team's defense.

Winger Pat Falloon is another underachieving player that Clarke and Barber took from another team and added to the Flyers. Falloon was drafted in the first round by the San Jose Sharks, second overall, in the 1991 draft. But he struggled with the Sharks. The word was that expectations were too high for the quiet Falloon. So Clarke traded two draft picks and a minor-league player to the Sharks for Falloon. The winger went on to tie his career-high of 25 goals in 1995–96 and become one of the Flyers' most consistent players. Dykhuis was never given an opportunity to show his stuff in Chicago. High expectations hampered Falloon in San Jose. Clarke and Barber used their knowledge of those situations to pry the players away in important trades. When Barber worked with Farwell, he had helped the Flyers get all-star forward Rod Brind'Amour away from the St. Louis Blues in exchange for three players, none of whom, in their new club, approached Brind'Amour's importance to his new team.

"Those are the kinds of players that you follow up on," Barber says, referring to players that might be stolen away from other teams in trades that help one team more than the other. "Any time you're traveling you're looking for information," Barber says. "You're talking to reporters. You're learning things and reporting them back to the team. If there are any talks going on about a player, we want to be part of that and try to get a deal done."

One scout who parlayed his hockey knowledge into a Stanley Cup was Neil Smith. Smith started his NHL management career as a scout with the New York Islanders. He moved to Detroit when Jim Devellano became general manager there in 1982 and eventually was promoted from pro scout to the club's director of minor-league operations. In 1985 Smith became Detroit's director of pro scouting and general manager of the American Hockey League's Adirondack Red Wings. After Adirondack won the AHL's championship in 1986 and again in 1989, Smith was hired by the New York Rangers to replace Phil Esposito as general-

manager. In 1994, the Rangers team that Smith built won the Stanley Cup, the club's first title in fifty-four years.

Kevin McDonald, a pro scout for the Rangers who works under Smith, scouts the NHL, the AHL, and the International Ice Hockey League. Mostly, McDonald studies the NHL teams in October and November so that the Rangers know how the other teams have changed during the off-season. He charts the matchups, such as which center will be on the ice when Wayne Gretzky or Mark Messier is out there.

"It's the lifestyle that I enjoy," says McDonald, a former public relations staffer for the Rangers. "It doesn't bother me. I'm thirty-one, I'm single. It's more fun than commuting into New York and working in an office all the time. I wanted a hockey job. I started in public relations and to me that's a service job. I wanted to work in hockey, and at least this is strictly a hockey job."

Keith Allen and Bill Barber, both members of the Hockey Hall of Fame, spent much of their careers scouting talent for the Philadelphia Flyers.

THE OFFICIALS.

"There doesn't seem to be a rapport with the players any more."

GARY DORNHOEFER

the next time you boo the referee, remember he's human, too. Bill McCreary loves golf and fishing. Gord Broseker played baseball in the Texas Rangers organization. Pat Dapuzzo is a karate enthusiast. No discussion of hockey would be complete without a mention of the referees and linesmen who work nearly as hard as the players and receive much more grief. Fans ofen forgive their favorite players for mistakes. Referees seldom receive such kindness.

"It was in Boston in 1976 and the Flyers were playing the Bruins in a preseason game," says Joe Watson, who was playing for the Flyers at the time. "Well, a brawl breaks out and seven of their guys and eight of ours guys get into this huge fight. The referee was Art Skov and he's calling penalties left and right. So I go up to him and say, 'Art, listen, you're throwing all our defensemen out. I'm the last one left. Don't do this to me.' But he just smiled and kept on sending guys off. It ended up that me and Billy Barber played defense, and I don't think Billy ever did that before or after that game."

A linesman's job includes dropping the puck on faceoffs, watching for offsides, and, most dangerous, breaking up the constant scraps.

Gary Dornhoefer says that too many referees these days get caught up in the glamour of the game. In the 1970s, he says, referees would joke with the players and interact with them during games. "These days, it seems to me that if you look at a referee cross-eyed you get a 10-minute misconduct penalty," Dornhoefer said. "There doesn't seem to be a rapport with the players any more."

In 1996, the NHL lost one of its most distinguished referees of the modern era. Andy van Hellemond ended a twenty-five-year career after officiating a league-record 1,474 regular-season games and 221 playoff games. Van Hellemond, who went on to become the senior vice president and director of hockey operations for the East Coast Hockey League, made eighteen appearances in the Stanley Cup cham-

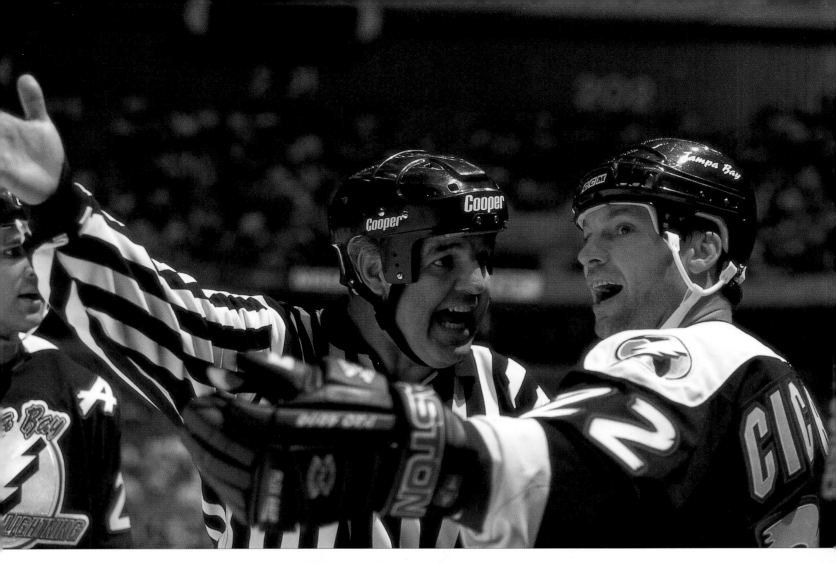

pionship series. Through the 1995–96 season, there were thirteen men in the Hockey Hall of Fame listed as either a referee or linesman, including Neil Armstrong who held the record for most games officiated before Van Hellemond with 1,314.

Florida Panthers president Bill Torrey contends that players should help out the referees by being more responsible with their sticks. Torrey says that the size and strength of players today makes it very dangerous to mishandle the stick. One wrong move and a serious head injury could occur. All players, except for Craig MacTavish, went into the 1996–97 season wearing a helmet. But it was not mandatory by the NHL.

"We always seem to look at the rules and the referees as being the cause or result of how a game is officiated. I think it's time, because they are a bigger factor in this, that the players themselves realize they are the biggest factor. They want to high-stick someone? They want to carry their sticks high? If they want to do certain things, if they don't respect who they're playing against, at a certain point you could have one hundred guys in the penalty box. So the players themselves dictate as much as the officials how the game is going to be played and officiated."

With players in the 1990s being generally more aggressive, the issue of high sticks became a hot topic among referees, players, and executives. "It's like raising the speed limit," Torrey says. "If the players respect their opponents, that's not going to be a factor. If they're going to use it to hook everybody in the neck, there's going to be problems. In the days before helmets, it you went after the other team's so-called skill players and high-sticked them or used your stick, I guarantee you there was a retaliation. Your guy was going to get it. It wasn't written in the rule book, but that's what you did. That's what happened."

Dino Ciccarelli gives it a good try, but it's doubtful he won this argugment with the referee. Ciccarelli had a career-high 138 penalty minutes in 1981–82.

Early History

"You always remember the first time you win the Stanley Cup."

SCOTTY BOWMAN,
Detroit Red Wings coach

Opposite: The 1993 Montreal Canadiens, led by goaltender Patrick Roy, won their first Stanley Cup since 1986 by rolling over Wayne Gretzky and the upstart Los Angeles Kings.

the Stanley Cup, originally called the Dominion Challenge Cup, may stand just three feet (90cm) tall, but every player who has ever hoisted it over his head and waltzed deliriously around the rink will tell you that it makes him feel ten feet tall.

Established in 1892 by Frederick Arthur, Lord Stanley of Preston, sixth governor general of Canada, and first awarded to amateur hockey teams in 1893, the Cup has become the greatest trophy in sports. It is the oldest trophy competed for by professional athletes in North America. Lord Stanley purchased the trophy for less than the cost of a single ticket in most NHL arenas these days, but its worth to today's players is inestimable. In no other sport does the championship team parade around the playing surface with the trophy over its collective heads. In no other sport does the championship trophy travel all over North America, make appearances on national television, and get ogled by starstruck fans whenever it is shown. And fascination with the Cup is nothing new. Teams from Winnipeg and Ottawa were engaged in a heated game in the 1904 series in

Ottawa when fire alarms were heard over the roar of the crowd. The post office was going up in flames, but no one wanted to leave the hockey game, including the firefighters. How could they leave? The Stanley Cup was at stake.

"The fans and the emotions in the buildings are incredible," says Ron Hextall, who went to the finals as a rookie with the 1987 and 1997 Philadelphia Flyers. "But you can't allow yourself to get caught up in it and get away from what's gotten you where you are. There is a thing about overpreparation and overpsyching yourself up."

In 1902, Toronto fans, waiting to hear how their team did out west against Winnipeg in the championship round, stayed awake long into the night, listening

Above: The Winnipeg Victorias battled powerhouse teams from Montreal, Toronto, and Ottawa for the Stanley Cup in the 1890s and early 1900s. The Vics were the pride of western Canada after they won Cups in 1896 and 1901.

The Toronto Maple
Leafs got to drink
from the Stanley Cup
for the third
straight season in
1964 by beating the
Detroit Red Wings in
seven gruelling
games.

for whistle blasts from the Toronto railway station. Two whistles indicated that
the local team had won; three blasts meant defeat. Alas, the Toronto Wellingtons
lost to the Winnipeg Victorias that year, and the sleepy fans had to endure three
long, sad whistles.

And to think that Lord Kilcoursie, Lord Stanley's aide, paid just 10 guineas—
$48.67 Canadian and $50 U.S.—for the original bowl, which today sits on a 35 ¼-
inch (90cm) pillar of silver bands that bear the names of the winners. Lord
Stanley never really knew the excitement his gift brought. He left Canada and
returned to England without seeing even one Stanley Cup playoff game.

Like the game it has come to represent, the Cup has undergone many
changes. In its infancy, the Cup was controlled by a pair of trustees designated by
Lord Stanley from 1893 to 1909—Otawa residents Sheriff John Sweetland and
Philip D. Ross—and competed for by teams in the Amateur Hockey Association
of Canada. The Montreal Amateur Athletic Association won the first Cup in
1893 by going 7–1 in a playoff series against two other teams from Montreal and
one each from Quebec and Ottawa. In a tradition that would eventually be

adopted by most other sports, the members of winning team received gold rings for their accomplishment.

Unlike in modern hockey, many teams in the late 1800s did not have regular schedules. Because they played on natural ice, they had to play their games between December and March, and the day-to-day weather often played a part in the scheduling. At first, any team could challenge the defending champions for possession of the Cup, and it was the job of the trustees to determine which teams had earned that right.

The rules began to change in 1910, when the National Hockey Association (NHA) was formed and immediately took control of the Cup competitions. Because the league was still small and teams came and went quite quickly, other leagues were encouraged to challenge the NHA champions for the championship trophy. The Ontario Professional Hockey League challenged the NHA several times, but it was the Pacific Coast Hockey Association (PCHA) that served as the toughest challenger. One of the more powerful leagues at the time, the PCHA challenged the NHA champions in 1914, 1915, and 1916. This rivalry continued until 1926, even when the NHL replaced the NHA in 1917.

As the professional game began to overtake the amateur game in popularity, amateur players began to resent their professional counterparts. So Sir Montague Allan of Montreal defused the tension by donating the Allan Cup in 1908 to serve as the new senior amateur championship trophy.

In 1926, when the PCHA lost most of its players to new NHL teams in New York, Chicago, and Detroit, the Stanley Cup playoffs became the tournament that we recognize today. From that season on, the Stanley Cup has been the exclusive championship trophy of the NHL. The Montreal Maroons were the last non-NHL team to win the trophy when they beat the Victoria Cougars in 1926.

Since 1918, the Montreal Canadiens have dominated the Stanley Cup playoffs. Through the 1995–96 season, the Canadiens had won twenty-three Cups, ten more than the Toronto Maple Leafs and sixteen more than the Detroit Red Wings. Eleven of the league's twenty-six teams have never won the Cup.

"It's really something else when it all gets down to one game," says Shawn Antoski, who played for the 1994 Vancouver team that lost in the finals to the

The Stanley Cup in 1902 was much smaller than the modern version. To inscribe the names of all the winners, large bands had to be added on the bottom.

Detroit Red Wings center Sergei Fedorov takes off on a break-away against the Philadelphia Flyers in the 1997 Stanley Cup finals. The Wings swept the Flyers in four games to win their first Cup since 1955.

Rangers. "It's one shift, one period, and let the chips fall where they may. If you want any game at home, it's Game Seven. When you have it in front of your own fans, it goes a long way."

The Stanley Cup playoffs have created hundreds of heroes. One of the earliest stars of the tournament was Frank McGee of the Ottawa Silver Seven. A great scorer who got off to a slow start in the 1905 championship series, McGee was so enraged at being criticized by the challenging Dawson City Klondikers that he poured in 14 goals in a 23–2 victory in Game Two of the 2-game series. McGee, who went on to score 63 goals in 22 Stanley Cup games, earned a place in hockey history's what-might-have-been department when he was killed at age thirty-four in World War I.

The Klondikers, however, continued to make news after that series. Unable to afford the trip home to the Yukon, they went on a 23-game tour to earn money for the journey. In the end, however, seventeen-year-old goalie Albert Forrest was forced to walk the final 350 miles all alone.

In 1907, an unknown hero saved the Cup from a watery grave. It seems that a fan of the Kenora Thistles was so angry that the challenging Montreal Wanderers had tried to add several ringers to their team that he stole the Cup and threatened to throw it into the Lake of the Woods. Fortunately, cooler heads prevailed. The Cup was rescued, the series was played, and Montreal won. Whether or not the ringers were permitted to play was not documented.

In the early 1900s, a player for the champion Ottawa Silver Sevens dared a teammate to throw the Cup into the Rideau Canal, and the Cup was so thrown. Fortunately, the canal was frozen over. All kinds of strange things have happened to the Cup. It was once used by an unknowing woman as a flowerpot. It got thrown into a cemetery during an argument between teammates. It was stolen by a fan during the finals in 1962 when his beloved Montreal Canadiens were losing to the Chicago Blackhawks.

Players and Coaches—and the Stanley Cup

Many of hockey's greatest moments have been during the playoffs. Literally dozens of individual stars have sparkled brightest during the postseason. Here are some of the highlights:

• Jack Marshall is the only skater to have played on four different Cup-winning teams. He won championships with the Winnipeg Victorias in 1901, Montreal AAA in 1902, the Montreal Wanderers in 1907 and 1910, and the Toronto Blueshirts in 1914.

• Goalie Harry Holmes also played on four Cup winners—with the 1914 Toronto Blueshirts, the 1917 Seattle Metropolitans, the 1918 Toronto Arenas and the 1925 Victoria Cougars.

• Eddie Gerard won consecutive championship rings from 1921 to 1923 with the Toronto St. Pats and the Ottawa Senators, and Claude Lemieux won Cups with New Jersey in 1995 and Colorado in 1996.

• In 1922, Frank Nighbor won the first Hart Trophy as the NHL's most valuable player. He also won four Stanley Cups with the Ottawa Senators and is credited with perfecting the poke check.

• Ottawa's Frank "King" Clancy played all six positions in a game on March 31, 1923. How talented was Clancy? In 1930 the Toronto Maple Leafs paid the Senators $35,000 for Clancy, the most money paid for a player up to that point.

• Montreal star Newsy Lalonde scored 27 goals in 29 Cup games from 1908 to 1926.

• In the 1926 Cup tournament, Lester Patrick, then the forty-four-year-old coach of the New York Rangers, was forced to strap on the goaltender's gear and play the second and third periods against the Montreal Maroons. Rangers goalie Lorne Chabot was injured early in the second period, and the Maroons would not allow the Rangers to pluck a reserve out of the stands. Teams were permitted to dress just one goaltender in those days. So Patrick himself jumped between the pipes, and the Rangers went on to win the game and the series, 3 games to 2.

King Clancy once played all six positions in a single game. Here he poses in his uniform for the Maple Leafs, who acquired him from the Senators.

• In 1951, Toronto's Bill Barilko scored the game-winning goal as the Maple Leafs beat the Montreal Canadiens in the Stanley Cup finals. Tragically, Barilko was killed in a plane crash that summer.

• In the 1952 Cup playoffs, goalie Terry Sawchuk and the Detroit Red Wings allowed an incredible average of only 0.63 goals per game as they powered to the title by winning the minimum 8 games. Sawchuk was so good that he did not allow a goal at home and surrendered just 5 in the entire tournament.

• Even though the Flyers lost to the Oilers in the 1987 finals, goalie Ron Hextall won the Conn Smythe Trophy by leading all goalies in games, minutes, and shutouts.

• Goalie Grant Fuhr won a record 16 games to lead the Oilers to the 1988 Cup.

• Wayne Gretzky scored a record 13 points in 4 games against the Boston Bruins in the 1988 finals. It was after the Oilers defeated the Bruins in this series that the custom of taking a team photograph of the champions was established.

• Mario Lemieux won back-to-back Conn Smythe Trophies in 1991 and 1992, recording 32 goals and 46 assists in 38 playoff games.

• In 1996 Colorado's Joe Sakic scored a playoff-high 18 goals and captured the Conn Smythe Trophy as the Avalanche won their first Stanley Cup.

"If you can't enjoy this time of year and this excitement, you can't enjoy the game at all," says Craig MacTavish, who, in addition to his three Stanley Cups with the Edmonton Oilers, added one with the New York Rangers in 1994. "It's so easy to prepare yourself for games that are so important. The adrenalin is right there. It makes playing the game that much easier. The enthusiasm from the young guys on the team is very infectious to the rest of us. It's exciting for me to see the excitement in their eyes and the way they're experiencing the playoffs and their first run at success."

The Florida Panthers' Ed Jovanovski experienced that thrill as a rookie in 1996 when the Panthers, an expansion team that had few believers early in the season, used a tough defense and opportunistic offense to roll past Boston, Philadelphia, and Pittsburgh to a date with Colorado in the finals.

Hall of Fame goal-
tender Terry Sawchuk
used his leg pads to
rack up 12 shutouts
in the NHL playoffs.
In 1967, he won the
Stanley Cup with the
Toronto Maple Leafs.

"Our goal was just to make the playoffs," says Jovanovski, who had 1 goal and 8 assists in the postseason tournament. "Then we hit some slumps. But we overcame those slumps and started playing well again. Seeing how the team got better and more confident in each playoff series proved to us that we could do it. All around the locker room the intensity was high, and I loved coming to the rink every day. You're playing well, the team is winning, and there was no complaints. You win together and lose together."

The Panthers did indeed play as a team in 1995–96. Right wing Scott Mellanby led the Panthers with 32 goals and 38 assists during the regular season, but four other players all chipped in at least 50 points. Dave Lowry led the Panthers with 10 playoff goals, while seven other players scored at least 4. "We played four lines all year long, and then we played them all in the playoffs, too," says Florida coach Doug MacLean. "Now there were a lot better teams with a much better first line than us. They might even have had a better top two, three, or four guys. But to play for eight months and win, it's not only the quality of the first line but also the quality of the fourth line and the third pair of defense."

"We all have a job to do," says Philadelphia Flyers goalie Ron Hextall. "There are twenty guys in the lineup, and everybody has to do their job. Hopefully, somebody will step up and play the game of their life. But it's about team, and it's about twenty guys stepping up. You grow from experiences like that."

"Players who want to be good players are good observers," says coach Terry Murray, who has coached both Washington and Philadelphia in the playoffs. "This is a special time of the year, and you have to observe what is going on. You have to work your way through the frustration, through the adversity, through the failure, and put it all together real fast."

Florida Panthers center Rob Niedermayer tries to stickhandle around Colorado Avalanche defenseman Alexei Gusarov in Game Four of the 1996 Stanley Cup finals. The Panthers lost four straight games to the Avalanche in their first finals appearance.

Many coaches also earned their fame in the Stanley Cup playoffs. The legendary Toe Blake, perhaps the greatest coach ever, led the Montreal Canadiens to five consecutive Cup titles from 1956 to 1960. Fred "the Fog" Shero took the Flyers to back-to-back Cups in 1974 and 1975. The inscrutable Scotty Bowman led the Canadiens to four consecutive titles from 1976 to 1979. Gentlemanly Al Arbour directed the New York Islanders to 4 straight championships from 1980 to 1983. And gritty Glen Sather's Edmonton Oilers won the Cup five times in seven seasons beginning in 1984.

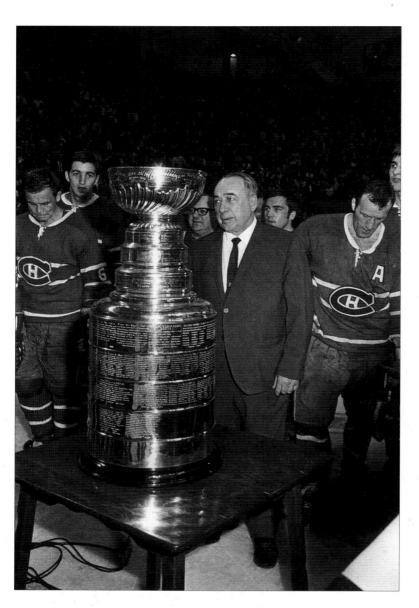

"Playing in the Stanley Cup playoffs is never a crap shoot," says Terry Murray. "It's a fire drill. It's organized. It's staying in line. It's marching out the door and knowing the direction you want to go. You've got to point your club's compass north and just head that way. When you get to the NHL and want to win the Stanley Cup, you have to become very interdependent on your teammates. That's a real mental development."

Three women have their names engraved on the Stanley Cup. They are Marguerite Norris, president of the Detroit Red Wings in 1955; Sonia Scurfield, the 1989 co-owner of the Calgary Flames; and Marie-Denise DeBartolo York, the 1991 president of the Pittsburgh Penguins.

Like all dramatic events, the Stanley Cup playoffs produced its share of rascals. Although they lost to their opposition in the NHA-PCHA playoffs, the 1915 Ottawa Senators, the 1916 Portland Rosebuds, and the 1917 Vancouver Millionaires engraved their names on the Cup after their league playoffs but before the final series.

In 1925, the Hamilton Tigers, instead of competing in the playoffs, went on strike for a pay raise and ended up being suspended and relocated the next season to New York as the Americans.

After the Victoria Cougars won the Cup in 1925, general manager and coach Lester Patrick stored the Cup in the basement of his home in Victoria, British Columbia. One day, Patrick's two sons, Muzz and Lynn, were fooling around in the basement and discovered the Cup. Being somewhat mischievous, the two boys carved their initials into the trophy with a nail.

At least the boys never lost the Cup. The same can't be said for the 1924 Montreal Canadiens. After being honored for their championship by the

In a dramatic ending to one of the NHL's greatest reigns, Toe Blake announced after winning the 1968 Stanley Cup that he was retiring as coach of the Montreal Canadiens.

University of Montreal, Georges Vezina, Sprague Cleghorn, Sylvio Mantha, and Leo Dandurand took the Cup on a short trip from the university to Dandurand's home. On the way, however, Dandurand's Model-T Ford developed engine trouble, and three of the men got out to push. Cleghorn, who was personally guarding the Cup, set it on the curb and joined his buddies in pushing the car up a hill. It wasn't until Dandurand's wife asked about the Cup some time later that night that the men realized they had left it on the curb. To their everlasting relief, the Cup was still there when the frantic men returned.

In 1994 the New York Rangers, led by their captain Mark Messier, took the Cup on several TV shows and to several bars, including a popular strip club where visitors and dancers alike fondled and cavorted with the pride of Lord Stanley. "I can still remember the exposure it got," says Kevin McDonald, a scout for the Rangers. "From the David Letterman show to *Good Morning America* and from MTV to Howard Stern. That Cup was all over New York."

Although the Colordo Avalanche kept the Cup in the United States for the third straight season—New Jersey won it in 1995 and the New York Rangers in 1994—it was the 1916 Portland Rosebuds who became the first U.S. team to play for the Cup. They didn't win, however, so the 1917 Seattle Metropolitans became the first U.S. team to claim the Cup.

In addition to the colorful men who played for the Cup, there were wild games nearly every year. The Toronto Maple Leafs and Boston Bruins had to suspend a game in the 1950–51 semifinals because their Saturday night overtime game carried them into Toronto's Sunday morning curfew. The Bruins were also involved in a crazy 3–3 game in the 1988 finals against the Edmonton Oilers. Game Four of the series had to be suspended in the third period when a power failure at the Boston Garden left the entire place in darkness.

When the end finally comes, it's exhilarating. Here, the New York Rangers celebrate at Madison Square Garden after beating the Vancouver Canucks in Game Seven of the 1994 Stanley Cup finals.

In 1919, the series between Montreal and Seattle was cancelled because of an outbreak of influenza. In 1968, the assassination of Dr. Martin Luther King, Jr. was cause for the postponement of three series of games during the quarterfinal round by a minimum of two days.

"You can't win the Stanley Cup unless you win the big games," says Craig MacTavish. "Very few times does the team that wins the Stanley Cup go through the playoffs without facing elimination. That's where you go through the environment that helps teams grow and get better."

"The only thing that really counts is the playoffs," says Rod Brind'Amour, who began his career with the St. Louis Blues and was later traded to Philadelphia. "You want to have a good year and get to the playoffs and then gear up for that. You can have a good year and not be good in the playoffs, and (the season) doesn't matter at all."

There is one thing that players and coaches all agree on. Enjoy the trip to the finals because you may never go back there again. "Anytime you can win, you win," says Bill Torrey, president of the Florida Panthers. "You don't say 'I'll put it off for a year.' You take everything you can get your hands on. Without the year we had in 1995–96 we might not have a new building to play in. We might not have even had a future in Florida. Our success was very, very important for solidifying our franchise in that market. It was important for the league, and it was important for our franchise."

Former Flyers coach Terry Murray says it's a big mistake to think that second chances come along every day. "You can't assume you'll be back, and you can't be so egotistical that you think anything like that," says Murray. "This is professional sports and anything can happen. There are no guarantees. There are no teams in this league that can have the Stanley Cup sitting on their desk in August heading into training camp. You've got to get lucky. You've got to get some bounces. You have to have some solid play from your top players to get there."

Goalie Ron Hextall points to the 1994–95 New York Rangers and Vancouver Canucks. The Rangers lost in the Eastern Conference semifinals the year after they won the Cup, and the Canucks lost in the Western Conference semifinals the year after they lost in the final to the Rangers.

"That's a prime example of what happens from year to year," says Hextall. "You have to take advantage of the situation you're in. It's a tough road every year. There are a lot of variables with injuries, guys having off years. When you're there, you have to take advantage of it."

While Mike Bossy was with the New York Islanders, his team won four Stanley Cups, and he remembers a little something from each one. "The first one was always special because it was the first one," says Bossy. "They each bring out a special little memory. The second one, my dad died two days after we won the Cup. The third one, I won the Conn Smythe. The fourth one was special beating the Oilers in four straight. They all have a little significance to them."

Left winger Pat Conacher was a part-time player for the Oilers when they won the Cup in 1984. He was also a key player on the 1993 Los Angeles Kings teams that went to the finals and lost to the Canadiens. That team featured Wayne Gretzky, Jari Kurri, Tomas Sandstrom, Luc Robitaille, Rob Blake, and Kelly Hrudey. The Kings finished third in their division that season but rolled all the way to the finals on an improbable journey.

"No one expected us to get there," Conacher says. "We just got cranked up and away we went. It was definitely the most rewarding thing personally to myself because I was an everyday player. They were expecting things from me, and I thought I was coming through for them. Going to the finals was just awesome. The big thing about that year was the three teams we beat out getting to the finals, against Montreal, were all Canadian teams. So every night in Canada I was on TV coast-to-coast and all my friends and family got to see me every night. That was a big thing for me."

The Kings beat Calgary and Vancouver, and the third series against Toronto went seven gruelling games, two won in overtime, before the Kings advanced on a 5–4 victory in Game Seven.

"All the hockey world wanted a Montreal-Toronto matchup in the end," says Conacher. "No one wanted the L.A. Kings. They wanted an old original six-team matchups, and the Toronto Maple Leafs did so well that year. Going back into Toronto for that seventh game was everything and more than the writers write about and the TV guys talk about. It was so much bigger than that just because of the Toronto fame and mystique. They were Canada's team. And they were counting Wayne Gretzky out. The media people and the world said that all the years in L.A., and he had never taken them to the promised land. He took it to another level in that Game Seven. The way we beat them that night, it was euphoria. It was just fantastic."

Unfortunately for Conacher and the Kings, Montreal goalie Patrick Roy led the Canadiens to the Cup in five games. "We played well in the games. We just didn't have enough," Conacher said. "Three of the five games were one-goal games, all in overtime. We fought extremely hard. It just wasn't enough to be beat them that year."

The next season, with club owner Bruce McNall in financial trouble, the Kings had to sell off many of their top players. After having high expecations, measuring up became too great of a weight to bear, and the Kings missed the playoffs and suffered a total letdown.

"It just goes to show you how hard it is to repeat in the league now," Conacher says. "If you're not prepared to play every night they want to knock the king off the mountain."

Gretzky played for the Kings for eight years but was never able to lead them to a Stanley Cup victory.

The Dynasties

"I don't know if I'll ever have another year like that. It doesn't happen that often."

DOUG MacLEAN,
Florida Panthers coach

they are the teams that captured our imaginations. They were no one-year wonders, whose passing through would soon be forgotten. These were the dynasties, the clubs that were built by general managers with foresight and led by coaches with staying power. The Detroit Red Wings, Montreal Canadiens, Toronto Maple Leafs, New York Islanders, and Edmonton Oilers were teams that dominated the NHL with explosive offenses, swarming defenses, and near-perfect goaltending. They all won Cup after Cup, and, maybe after a miss, another one or two Cups after that. They all had stars—Howe, Richard, Mahovlich, Bossy, Gretzky—and they all had players who rose to the occasion.

"That's the way the playoffs are," says Craig MacTavish, who played for three Cup winners with Edmonton. "It's difficult. The checking gets tighter, and the competition gets stiffer. It's tough to score in those situations. That's why you see so many times in the history of the playoffs a lot of the so-called unheralded players come up big. That's what you need to win Stanley Cups."

The Detroit Red Wings, 1950–55

After losing in the finals in 1948 and 1949, the Detroit Red Wings finally won Stanley Cups in 1950, 1952, 1954, and 1955. Led by Gordie Howe, Ted Lindsay, Sid Abel, Terry Sawchuk, and Red Kelly, the Red Wings won seven consecutive regular-season titles during their run. In 1950, Lindsay, Abel, and Howe finished first, second, and third, respectively, in scoring. Detroit's 1950 run to the Cup was marred by an injury to Howe that almost ruined his career. Playing against Toronto in Game One of the semifinals, Howe tried to check the Maple Leafs' Ted Kennedy near the Red Wings' bench. Kennedy pulled up abruptly, however, and Howe plowed face-first into the boards. He suffered a concussion, a broken nose, a fractured right cheekbone, and a scratched eyeball.

Even without Howe, the Wings went on to beat the Leafs and then

Toronto goalie Harry Lumley's face shows the fear the Maple Leafs must have felt when facing the Red Wings in the 1954 semifinals.

the New York Rangers, who had to play their home games in the finals in Toronto because the circus was at Madison Square Garden.

After losing to Montreal in the 1951 semifinals, the Wings roared back in 1952 to sweep Toronto in the semifinals and Montreal in the finals. That team, which featured the "Production Line" of Howe, Abel, and Lindsay, allowed just 5 goals in the playoffs and was considered one of the best teams in NHL history. Jack Adams, who served as general manager of the Wings from 1927 to 1963, was credited for putting together the dynasty.

The Montreal Canadiens, 1956–60

The Canadiens, in what many call the greatest dynasty of them all, dominated the NHL so thoroughly from 1956 to 1960 that they won five consecutive Stanley Cups and had the best regular-season record in four of those seasons. It was after the 1955–56 season that the NHL, so overpowered by the Canadiens' power play, changed the rule to allow penalized players to return to the ice after the first

Montreal's Claude Provost and Doug Harvey play defense against Detroit's Gordie Howe and a leaping Ted Lindsay in the fourth game of the 1956 Stanley Cup finals. Jacques Plante, the goalie for the Canadiens, shut out the Red Wings and helped lead Montreal to its first Stanley Cup.

power-play goal was scored. That rule had to be made because the Canadiens, led by Rocket Richard, Boom Boom Geoffrion, and Doug Harvey, scored again and again on its power play and ran over teams unmercifully. Coach Toe Blake did a masterful job of turning a team dotted with both veterans and youngsters into a cohesive unit for half a decade. The unpredictable Jacques Plante won the Vezina Trophy as the NHL goaltender with the best goals-against average all five seasons during the Cup run, and Harvey won the Norris Trophy as the league's best defenseman four times. Along the front line, the brothers Richard—Maurice and Henri—joined Dickie Moore, Jean Beliveau, Geoffrion, and Bert Olmstead to form two of the greatest scoring lines in hockey history. Their aggressive push to the net was dubbed "Firewagon" hockey, and all goal-scoring-crazy clubs were nicknamed that thereafter.

The Toronto Maple Leafs, 1962–67

The Toronto Maple Leafs were the clutch team of the 1960s. The Leafs won just one regular-season title during their four-Cup run, and they didn't have the collection of superstars that other great teams had. But they won when they had to, and that's the mark of a great team. The fiery Punch Imlach, coach and general manager, was an energetic motivator, and it was under him that Johnny Bower resurrected his career as a goalie. Allan Stanley and Tim Horton became stars with the Leafs, and Red Kelly made an impressive switch from defenseman to center. The scoring line of Dave Keon, Dick Duff, and George Armstrong was

A good defense is key to winning championships. Here, the Toronto Maple Leafs do a fine job of keeping the Montreal Canadiens away from the net.

complemented by another potent trio of Kelly, Frank Mahovlich, and Bob Nevin. The Leafs beat Detroit twice and Chicago and Montreal each once on their way to four titles in six years. The Leafs, who won the Cup in 1962, 1963, 1964, and 1967, won their first regular-season title in fifteen years in 1963. The Leafs were so balanced that season that five different players went on to record multiple-goal games against the Red Wings in the finals. In 1964, Sawchuk, bothered by a pinched nerve in his shoulder, left his hospital bed to return to the team and lead them to a 7-game victory over Chicago.

The Montreal Canadiens, 1976-79

How's this for dominance? During the time they won their four consecutive Stanley Cup titles from 1976 to 1979, the Canadiens won 16 of 19 playoff games in the finals. Against the Rangers in the 1979 finals, they did not allow more than 25 shots in any game. In one of the most dominating seasons ever, the Canadiens went 60–8–12 in 1976–77. Although winger Guy Lafleur was scoring goals by the bushel and coach Scotty Bowman was weaving his motivational magic, the Canadiens were driven by four defensemen—Larry Robinson, Serge Savard, Guy Lapointe, and Bob Gainey. That quartet provided such a strong defense that

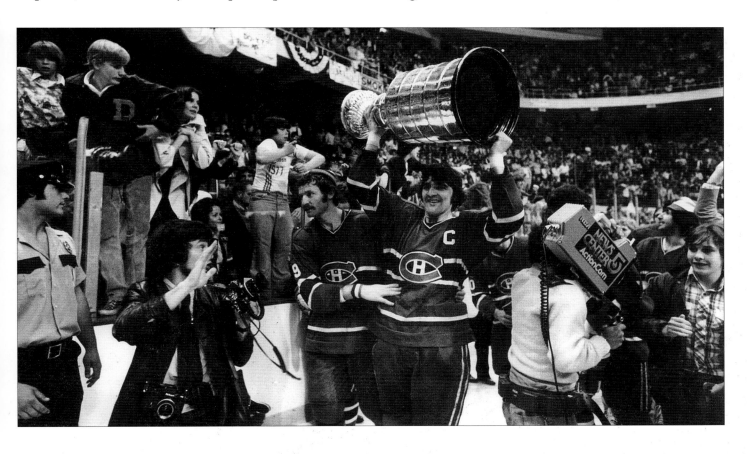

goalie Ken Dryden went on to become one of the most productive goalies ever. A finesse team that could fight if it had to, the Canadiens ended the two-year reign of the Philadelphia Flyers by knocking off the rollicking two-time Cup champions in the 1976 finals.

Coach Scotty Bowman remembers that beating the Flyers was a highlight of that run for him. "I remember the first time we won the Cup in Montreal real well and maybe the last one in Montreal," says Bowman. "Of all the five Cups we won in Montreal we only won one actually in Montreal. And I remember the year we knocked the Flyers off. It was a big and exciting time for us, because they had won it two years in a row, and we won it in four straight—two in Philadelphia, a pretty tough place to play—and they were a good team. That was when our team really came together. We went on to win three more after that."

"Just my time I spent with that group of guys was great," says Larry Robinson. "It was a very interesting group that had a lot of talent. One of the thrills was the year we beat the Flyers. They had a terrific team at that time, and they had just won a couple of Stanley Cups. So to be able to beat them twice in their own building, where they had Kate Smith singing the National Anthem, was pretty exciting."

Star defenseman Serge Savard carried the Stanley Cup as Larry Robinson stayed close after the Canadiens swept the Bruins in Boston in the 1977 finals.

The New York Islanders, 1980–83

Perhaps the most complete team ever assembled, the New York Islanders won four consecutive Stanley Cups under general manager Bill Torrey and coach Al Arbour. The Islanders had scorers in Mike Bossy, Bryan Trottier, and Denis Potvin. They had fighters in Clarke Gilles and Bobby Nystrom. They had goalie Billy Smith. They had inspirational players like John Tonelli, Butch Goring, and John Tonelli, and they used all that talent to win 19 straight playoff series before losing to Edmonton in the 1984 finals.

"It was a unique run when you think about it," says Torrey. "Everybody mentions all the Cups, but to me, and I was just talking to Al Arbour about this the other day, we won 19 consecutive playoff series. That to me is something that is going to take some doing in this modern day and age to do again. The best part about that group of players was that, in spite of the number of guys who were big stars—Trottier, Bossy, all those guys—not that they were off-ice bosom buddies every day, but once they walked into a building whatever we set down as the way to go, whatever Al wanted them to do, they did it and blended it all together very well. Obviously at times certain guys would be asked to do certain things that probably they didn't want to do at the time. But if you don't have those role players in support like that you can't sustain the success. It's too easy to bring down one or two guys. The reason we were successful was because—if you go back and look at the records—guys who maybe weren't first-team All-Stars were guys who were major contributors. They all had a big role."

One player who had a big role was defenseman Kenny Morrow. Morrow was labeled by Torrey as one of the most underrated players ever to play in the NHL, and having him on the team allowed Torrey to trade defenseman Dave Lewis in the deal that brought Butch Goring to the team. In 1980, Morrow was a member of the U.S. Olympic team. "I watched Kenny Morrow at Lake Placid for two weeks play against some of the best players in the world and handle it like a seasoned veteran," says Torrey. "Yet he was a twenty-two-year old college kid with a beard."

Because of the versatility that Arbour and his players had, the Islanders could match up against anybody. "If it was a run-and-gun game, fine. We'd run and gun with you," says Torrey. "If you wanted to play shut-it-down and try to win, 1–0, we'll shut her down and we'll win 1–0. If you wanted to try to kick the stuffing out of us like the Bruins did that one series, we fought like alley cats for 5 games. The biggest weakness that we had was defense, and that's the most important thing for a team. It's probably the most difficult thing to get, too. Defensemen are not easy to come by. When I brought Al in, I knew I was drafting Denis Potvin. I drafted Davey Lewis. I took Bert Marshall in the interleague draft that year off the Rangers. Gerry Hart carried over. So what I wanted to do was knock 100 goals off our goals-against total. We had the worst goals-against in our first year as an expansion team. It was terrible. So we had big changes on our defense, and I wanted somebody that was really strong in coaching from the defense out.

"That's the one thing that Al was on them every day about. They had to be able to handle whatever was thrown at them on any given night, and when you're expected to win, you have to expect teams to throw different scenarios at you, and you have to be able to handle it. Really good teams are not just one-dimensional."

Most players never get to hoist the Stanley Cup over their heads. Mike Bossy, shown here in 1983, was able to carry the trophy four times with the New York Islanders.

The Edmonton Oilers, 1984–90

The greatest goal scorers in NHL history, the Edmonton Oilers poured in more than 400 goals in a season five times during their heyday, topping out at 446 in 1984. Led by a group of scorers that included Wayne Gretzky, Jari Kurri, Mark Messier, and Paul Coffey, the Oilers won five Stanley Cups in seven years. Perhaps most impressive was the Oilers' depth. They won their fourth Cup in 1988 after Coffey had been traded and their fifth in 1990 after Gretzky had been dealt. While the Big Four scored goals up front, goaltender Grant Fuhr was the backbone of the defense. Kevin Lowe provided the Oilers with a solid defenseman. The most important element of the team, however, may have been the coaching of Glen Sather. He was able to take a group of offensive wizards, add a half dozen tough guys to protect the scorers, and mix in a sampling of Europeans to come up with the perfect recipe for success. Sather was also able to add new players to the mix after Coffey and Gretzky left. Even after all the success of the early years, Sather managed to wind up with such stars as Adam Graves and Joe Murphy on his roster.

"They let those players think," Conacher says. "They did what came natural to them. Glen Sather let those guys go and play with creativity. They had built the idea into their team that there was always a backup, always support for someone."

"Being able to play on all those winning teams was so great," Kurri says. "You learn a lot by playing on those teams. You learn that it's a long year and that you can't put yourself down. You learn what it takes to stay on top of your game year after year. And when you get that winning feeling, you realize how much fun it is to play and win."

Only Montreal, Toronto, and Detroit have won more Stanley Cups than the Edmonton Oilers. Here team captain Mark Messier raises the Cup after winning the 1989–90 championship.

Dynasties to Come?

In recent years, different teams have won the Stanley Cup. The Detroit Red Wings won their first Cup since 1955 in 1997 by sweeping the Flyers in four games. After relocating from Quebec before the 1995–96 season, the Colorado Avalanche defeated the Florida Panthers in 4 straight games to win the Cup in 1996. The New Jersey Devils, who missed the playoffs altogether in 1996, used a stifling defense to defeat the heavily favored Detroit Red Wings in 4 straight games in 1995. The New York Rangers beat Vancouver in that dramatic 7-game series in 1994. And the Montreal Canadiens, under coach Jacques Demers, won their twenty-third Cup in 1993 by beating Wayne Gretzky and the Los Angeles Kings in 5 games. The only team to win back-to-back Cups since the Edmonton Oilers in 1987 and 1988 was the Pittsburgh Penguins, who used the talents of Mario Lemieux and Jaromir Jagr to beat Minnesota in 1991 and the Chicago Blackhawks in 1992.

Avalanche goaltender Patrick Roy celebrates victory after Game One of the 1996 finals against the Panthers with teammate Mike Keane. Roy has won three Stanley Cup championships.

Demers vividly recalls the thrill of winning in 1993. "When I came in there they had gotten beaten out by Boston in 4 games the previous year and I said I would get the team out of the division playoffs. That was tough living up to that. I certainly never promised the Stanley Cup. It was a dream for me. We had twenty-seven players, and when I had to sit out a guy like Denny Savard, that was difficult. But I made the commitment, as did the players, that we'd all stick together and work for the same goal. And we did that.

"Once you get to the conference finals and the Stanley Cup, there is no problem getting the players up. I've always been a positive person, and when you're positive you can bring that to the players. I told them in March that we were going to shock the hockey world. They didn't know what I was saying, but I believed it. And once you start making the players believe it you're halfway there. As good as Patrick Roy was as our goalie that year, we made sure the players knew it was going to be a team effort that was going to win for us."

The Losers

n o look at the Stanley Cup playoffs would be complete without a look at the losers. With an 82-game season to play and four rounds of playoffs, just getting to the finals is an accomplishment. But no one remembers the losers except the players themselves. They all say that the trip to the finals means nothing unless they win. Just getting to the most anticipated and most watched series of the season is certainly an experience and an accomplishment, but just getting there doesn't quite satisfy.

"You can't make an issue out of just getting to the finals," says coach Doug MacLean, who took the expansion Florida Panthers to the 1996 finals against Colorado and lost in 4 consecutive games. Led by the fantastic goaltending of John Vanbiesbrouck, the Panthers rolled over Boston, Philadelphia, and Pittsburgh to get to the big show. "The players all felt really good about getting there," says MacLean. "Everybody knows how hard it is to go the finals. It's everybody's goal, but we looked at a lot shorter goals than that during the season. So many things have to happen no matter how good you are. So many things have to fall into place. We were thrilled with the accomplishment, but you have to start at zero points again the next year."

Panthers defenseman Terry Carkner said that losing to the Avalanche in 4 straight games was very disheartening. The victory in the Eastern Conference finals over Mario Lemieux and the Pittsburgh Penguins turned out to be the highlight of Carkner's playoffs. "From that point on, it was pretty well down hill," says Carkner. "We got patted on the back a lot for getting that far, but we lost the last 4 games of the year. So there wasn't a lot to really be happy about."

Florida Panthers defenseman Robert Svehla slashes winger Claude Lemieux to keep him away from the puck in Game Four of the 1996 Stanley Cup finals. Lemieux scored five goals in 19 playoff games that year.

The Rangers' Fifty-Four-Year Wait

They called it the Curse of the New York Rangers, and it seemed more fact than fiction for fifty-four long years. When the Rangers beat the Vancouver Canucks to win the 1994 Stanley Cup, Rangers fans celebrated as much for the end of the Curse as they did for the team's achievement. Before the Rangers beat the Canucks in 7 gruelling games, they had gone fifty-four seasons without a Stanley Cup victory; this was longer than a lifetime for some and certainly the longest stretch of futility at the time.

This futility was no accident, and it was believed by some of the Rangers faithful that this string of bad luck resulted from an event that happened after the Rangers beat the Toronto Maple Leafs in 6 games in 1940 to win their third championship. That was also the year that the Madison Square Garden Corporation paid off a $3 million mortgage on the Garden. To celebrate the company's fulfillment of their debt, the board of directors, led by General John Reed Kilpatrick, got up early one January morning in 1941 and burned the actual mortgage in the bowl of the Stanley Cup. Grainy pictures show a smiling Kilpatrick dropping the paper into the Cup as the other directors, wearing black ties and tails, look on happily.

Hockey people, superstitious by nature, were stunned. How dare the group of businessmen use their Cup as a fireplace to burn a financial document! Players drank champagne from that Cup. They danced with it around the rink after their labors resulted in the ultimate victory. To have the Cup desecrated with fire and paper was a disgrace, and Lester Patrick, then the general manager of the Rangers, was worried that such an obviously materialistic act would result in the Rangers never again possessing the sport's greatest treasure.

For fifty-three years it seemed that Patrick was right. In 1950 the Rangers went to the Cup finals and faced off against the Detroit Red Wings. The series was expected to be one of the best ever. The Rangers featured Don "Bones" Raleigh and goaltender Chuck Raynor, and the Red Wings were led by Jimmy McFadden and Pete Babando, one of the few Americans in the league. But the Rangers had a big problem. The Ringling Brothers circus was in New York at the same time that the Cup series was set to begin, and the circus had more clout than the NHL in those days. So the Rangers had to play their home games at another arena. After the Red Wings won Game One of the series at their Olympia Stadium, the Rangers finally settled on Toronto's Maple Leaf Gardens as their "home" rink. The teams split the 2 games there, and the Rangers won

New York Rangers forward Bryan Hextall (left), goaltender Dave Kerr (center), and coach Frank Boucher enjoy the party after beating the Toronto Maple Leafs in the 1940 Stanley Cup finals. New York would wait fifty-four years for another Stanley Cup.

Games Four and Five back in Detroit. Things looked good for New York at that point, and Game Six was scheduled to be held in Toronto. In those days, however, a deciding game of the finals could not be played at a neutral rink, so the Rangers were forced to play Games Six and Seven back in Detroit.

That's when the Curse reared its head. The Red Wings won Game Six by scoring twice in the third period and Game Seven when Babando beat Raynor on a thirty-five-footer (10.5m) in overtime.

The Rangers' luck was no better in 1972, when they played the Boston Bruins. The Bruins won the opener, 6–5, in a barnburner. Boston won again, this time 2–1, in the second game. The Rangers won Game Three, but the Bruins bounced back to win Game Four by a goal. Bobby Rousseau scored twice to lift the New Yorkers to a victory in Game Five. But the Bruins got 2 goals from Wayne Cashman and a shutout from goalie Gerry Cheevers to win the Cup at Madison Square Garden, 4 games to 2.

The Rangers made it back to the Cup finals in 1979, but they had the misfortune to meet up with the Canadiens and coach Scotty Bowman. At first, it

appeared that the Rangers had a chance to wipe out the Curse. They beat the Canadiens, who were coming off a gruelling semifinal series against Boston, in Game One. But that was to be the high point of the series for the Rangers. They lost Game Two, 6–2, and never regained the momentum. Montreal went on to win the next 3 games and its fourth consecutive Cup.

Of course, when the Rangers marched past the New York Islanders, the Washington Capitals, and the New Jersey Devils to take on the Canucks in the 1994 finals, New York was abuzz with thoughts of the Curse again. Rangers fans were confident that finally 1994 would be the year the team broke the dry spell because the Rangers had managed to get past the pesky Devils in a pair of dramatic overtime games, Game Three at the Garden and Game Six at the Meadowlands. Before that dramatic Game Three, Rangers captain Mark Messier, inadvertently by most counts, promised a win. Then he went out and delivered a hat trick in the third period for a 4–2 Rangers victory.

But getting by the Canucks would take more than luck. Led by goalie Kirk McLean and wingers Pavel Bure and Trevor Linden, Vancouver won the first game of the finals, 3–2, in overtime. Then the Rangers' offense, which was spearheaded by defenseman Brian Leetch and forwards Messier, Adam Graves, and Alexei Kovalev, got heated up. The Rangers outscored the Canucks 12–4 in the next 3 games to take a commanding 3-games-to-1 lead in the best-of-7 series. But the Curse wouldn't go away. Vancouver won Games Five and Six to send the teams back to Madison Square Garden for Game Seven.

Tuesday, June 14, 1994, will forever be remembered in New York as the Day the Curse Was Lifted. Coach Mike Keenan gave an inspiring speech in the dressing room before the game, and the fans in the packed arena exchanged lucky horseshoes and rabbit's feet. Leetch scored the game's first goal for the Rangers in the first period, and the Garden shook with excitement. The fans nearly tore the house down when Graves gave the Rangers a 2–0 lead late in the period. Linden scored for Vancouver to cut the lead to 2–1 in the second period. But Messier scored what would eventually be the winning goal later in the period as the Rangers went on to beat the Canucks, 3–2, and end the Curse forever.

"The Rangers-Vancouver series was just outstanding," says Brian Burke. "There was good drama in most of the games. There weren't a lot of blowouts. It was fun to watch each game, and I'm still a huge fan of the game. They were exciting. They were close. The skill level was high. The intensity was awesome. The goaltending was good. There wasn't one thing that I wanted to see differently."

The celebration at the end of the game seemed to go on forever. Leetch won the Conn Smythe Trophy as the most valuable player of the playoffs, and NHL commissioner Gary Bettman ended the Rangers' fifty-four-year frustration by saying, "Your long wait is over."

Although Leetch won the award as the best player of the playoffs, it was Messier who was the heart and soul of that Rangers team. He not only scored the Cup-winning goal, but also set a club record of 12 goals in one playoff year. He scored a point in each of his first 13 playoff games that spring and in 21 of 23 playoff games altogether. His goal on April 13 against the Islanders in the Eastern Conference quarterfinals moved him past Glenn Anderson and into third place on the NHL's all-time playoff goal scoring list.

According to Kevin McDonald, a scout for the Rangers in 1996 and a public relations staffer in 1994, Messier was more than simply a great player. He was

New York City's long-suffering fans honored the Rangers with a ticker tape parade after they beat the Vancouver Canucks in the 1994 Stanley Cup finals.

the leader the Rangers had been seeking ever since they bowed out of the Cup finals in 1979. "When he came here one of the first things he did was rearrange the locker room," says McDonald. "We used to have big Gatorade jugs in the middle of the room on a table that players could walk over to and get drinks from. But they blocked the view of the players from one side of the room to the other. Well, Mess made us move them so he could have eye contact with everyone in the whole room right from his stall. He wanted to see what each player was doing, and he wanted them to be able to seem him and each other. He always did little things like that. He got this picture that had a Vince Lombardi saying on it that was titled 'What it takes to be a winner' and he put it on the wall so that every player would see it every time he was in the room. He just brought that whole aura of winning that was never there before. He taught us how to win. And it wasn't only that we were going to win, but here's what you have to do to achieve it.

"People like Tony Amonte, a young guy like that, [Messier] helped his career so much. He showed him what you have to do. We'd be done with practice and Mark would say, 'OK, now it's time to ride the bike.' The guys would just stare at him. He was so organized. On New Year's Eve, he'd get the whole team to go out together to have a drink before they went their separate ways. They'd all have to go golfing in L.A. at the club he and Wayne Gretzky played at. In 1995, when Darren Langdon was called up from the minors, Mess had the trainer take his measurements, and he bought him a new suit. When Langdon came in there was a suit in his stall. He does so many things above and beyond."

Although the Rangers had finally won the Cup and ended the Curse, it would be a long time before things settled down at the Garden. There was plenty of off-ice trouble just ahead. Coach Mike Keenan and Rangers general manager Neil Smith never really got along. Smith was low-key and suave, a team player. Keenan was boisterous and demanding, out to win at all costs. So when Keenan wanted to leave the Rangers to work as coach and general manager of the St. Louis Blues, the Rangers let him go.

McDonald remembers that the relationships between Smith and Keenan and between Keenan and the players was extremely tense, but, he says, the relationships worked.

"It was a case of being on edge every day," says McDonald. "Whether it was Mike and Neil's relationship or Mike's and the players, or some of Mike's, what I call orchestrated, moves. Banging the stick on the cross bar at practice or calling a player in for a one-on-one. You were always on the edge. At the same time, I think everybody in the whole organization felt they had a great chance to win. That's how everybody got through it."

Many people associated with the Rangers that season said that Smith made the relationship with Keenan work because he knew that Keenan had the personality to force the Rangers to be winners. Keenan had taken teams in Philadelphia and Chicago to the finals, so his track record was solid. "I think Neil made it work by sacrificing himself," says McDonald. "He took the backseat to Mike. He took an unconfrontational role. That was Neil's best attribute." Keenan, on the other hand, planned to challenge the Rangers from the very start of the season. When the team lost its first preseason game against the cross-town Islanders that year, Keenan bellowed at the post-game press conference, "This team is not good enough to win the Stanley Cup."

"Then he rattled off about four or five reasons why," McDonald says. McDonald looked over at his boss, Barry Watkins, and mouthed silently, "This ain't going to be easy." "From there, the tone was set," says McDonald. "Later, when Neil left the coaches' room, he was assaulted by the media. They all said, 'Mike said this and that and what's your reaction?' From that day on, it was always like a chess match. There were great checks and balances. They each made the other one work a lot harder."

The International Game

hockey has been played by teams that represent nations from around the world ever since the game became organized back in the late 1800s. It was featured at both the first Winter Olympics and the World Championships in 1924.

With Canada being credited as the birthplace of hockey, it's understandable that it should dominate the worldwide game. As the NHL was getting underway in 1917, the International Ice Hockey Federation (IIHF) was developing, and Canada was taking a leading role in that development. The Canadians entered the international arena at the 1920 Olympics in Antwerp, Belgium, and won the gold medal. The Canadians won the 1924 gold medal, too, outscoring their opponents, 110–3. The United States, which would later pull off the Miracle on Ice (their defeat of the longtime champion Olympic team: the Russians) during the 1980 Olympics, snapped Canada's gold-medal streak in 1933. Despite this, the Canadians continued to dominate international play until 1954. By that time, the Soviet Union had nearly perfected their national team training, and they began making noises.

Even though Canada began putting together a national team in the early 1960s (earlier international tournaments had featured club teams), the Soviets went on to control the international game. In 1969, sick and tired of losing to the Soviets, the Canadians reorganized and established Hockey Canada to train their national team. That team played in the famous 8-game Summit Series in 1972 against the Soviets, which they won with a goal by Paul Henderson. Since then, Canada has flourished in the international setting. Between 1982 and 1995 the Canadians had won 9 World Junior Championships and 6 of 7 since 1990. Team Canada won the silver medal at the 1994 Olympics and the gold medal at the 1994 World Championships.

In 1960, perhaps taking a cue from their Canadian counterparts, the United States got off to a solid start in international play and solidified its program for good. The Americans had played teams from Canada in the late 1800s as the game was growing along the northern border, but the first real international game wasn't played until the 1920 Olympics at Antwerp, when the first international hockey hero of the United States, Hall of Famer Francis "Moose" Goheen, carried the boys in red, white, and blue to a silver medal. At the 1932 Olympics in Lake Placid, New York, an American team comprised wholly of men from

Above: The Soviet Union eliminated Canada and won the gold medal at the 1972 Olympics.

Opposite: Canada's Russ Courtnall hits the ice in front of Czechoslovakia's Radoslav Svoboda in the 1984 Olympics. Czechoslovakia won the silver medal that year.

Massachusetts won the silver medal. But it was the 1960 Olympics at Squaw Valley, California, that really kicked the American game into high gear.

During that year's Winter Games, goaltender Jack McCartan spurred the Americans to victories over Canada and the Soviet Union, leading the upstart hosts to win the gold medal. The country's first hockey craze erupted after that, and young players began flocking to leagues in Minnesota and Massachusetts. The U.S. Olympic team, which featured future NHL star Mark Howe, won the silver medal in 1972, but the real shining moment in the history of American hockey was yet to come. In 1980, back at Lake Placid, the United States upset Russia, 4–3, in the semifinals of an Olympic series that became known as the Miracle on Ice. Mike Eruzione, at the high point of his hockey career, scored the winning goal midway through the third period, sending the Americans into the gold-medal game against Finland. The Americans won that anticlimactic contest, 4–2. How good was that American team? Eleven of them went on to become regulars in the NHL. The United States went on to win the 1996 World Cup but finished out of the medals in the 1998 Olympics.

While the United States, Canada, and Russia have long been the best-known hockey countries on the international scene, hockey certainly was played—and played well—in numerous other nations. Czechoslovakia (now the Czech Republic) was prime hockey country in the early 1900s. A man named Josef Gruss is said to have translated the Canadian rules into his own language, and the Czechoslovakian Hockey Union was established in 1908. The Czechs dominated early play in Europe, winning championships in 1911, 1914, 1922, 1925, and 1929. But they were outclassed by the Canadians and Americans at the 1920

Olympics. By 1931 hockey was entrenched in the country. An artificial ice rink was unveiled that year in Prague, and forty-eight teams and more than one thousand players were featured in half a dozen organized leagues. When the Soviets began to dominate international play in the 1960s, the Czechs were right there with them. There were more than 970 teams and 65,000 players in Czech leagues in 1978. In 1996 the Czech Republic beat Canada, 4–2, to win the World Championship. Jaroslav Drobny was the first European player to be on an NHL club's reserve list (he was held on reserve in 1949 with the Boston

Bruins, but he never played in the league). The Tatra's Cup, one of the oldest tournaments in Europe, along with Switzerland's Spengler Cup, began in Czechoslovakia in 1929. Thanks to a goal by defenseman Petr Svoboda and great goaltending by Dominik Hasek, the Czech Republic beat Russia, 1-0, to win the 1998 Olympic gold medal.

How cold is it in Finland? This country, which held its first official game in Helsinki in 1899, has 115 indoor hockey arenas, only twenty-five of which have

Opposite: The 1994 Olympics brought some of the strongest teams together for international play. Here Slovakia takes on Canada.

Above: No wonder men wore hats in those days. The games were played outdoors at the 1932 Olympics at Lake Placid, New York.

artificial ice. But cold alone is not enough to foster the growth of great hockey players. The Finns struggled at first with the new game. They lost to Sweden, 8–1, in their first international game in 1928. In 1933 they played their first international road game and lost again to Sweden, 11–1. Finally in 1937 Finland beat Estonia, 2–1, for its first international victory. But things went downhill from there—they went 0–5–0 in the 1939 World Championship. Finland didn't win its first gold medal until the 1995 World Championship, when it beat Sweden, 4–1. At the 1998 Olympics, Finland beat Canada, 3-2, to win the bronze medal. Finland's most well-known player in the NHL is right winger Jari Kurri, a former teammate of Wayne Gretzky with the Oilers and Kings and one of the best ever to play the game.

Although Germany, like Finland, got off to a slow start as far as winning games was concerned, the country embraced hockey early. The Germans list their first official game as being played on February 4, 1897, on Lake Halensee in Berlin. Along with Belgium, Bohemia, England, Switzerland, and France, Germany was a member of the International Ice Hockey Federation in 1901. As of 1996, the country listed 331 teams and 26,000 players in fifteen leagues.

Unlike the European countries, the Soviet Union got off to a late start in the hockey rink. It wasn't until 1945 that a group of students from the Moscow College of Physical Education put on a demonstration of this strange new game called hockey. However, it didn't take long for the Soviets to learn the game. The first Soviet national championship game was played on December 22, 1946, and things snowballed from there. Learning the game from the Czechs and the Finns, the Soviets joined the IIHF in 1952 and shocked the world by winning the gold medal at the 1954 World Championship in Stockholm. By 1963 the Soviets were vying with Canada for the title of world's best hockey team. They won their first of nine consecutive World and European championships in 1963 and sent teams on a tour of North America for the first time in 1975. In 1989 goalie Vladislav Tretiak, a star of the Soviet National and the Central Red Army teams, became the first non–North American player to be inducted into the Hockey Hall of Fame. The Russians captured the silver medal at the 1998 Olympics by losing to the Czech Republic in the championship game.

Although the first skating associations in Slovakia were formed in 1871, the first organized hockey game wasn't played until 1921. Like the Soviets, the Slovaks were impressed by their neighbor's hockey prowess. When Czechoslovakia won the 1925 European Championships, the game's popularity soared in Slovakia. At the 1994 Olympics, Slovakia beat Canada, Italy, and France to go 3–0–2 in the opening round. They lost to Russia, 3–2, in a quarterfinal playoff game.

As for Sweden, we would expect that hockey would be embraced early—and we wouldn't be wrong. On January 31, 1921, more than two thousand fans showed up in chilly Stockholm, where they watched the Swedes beat the Germans, 4–1, in Sweden's first official game. The Swedish League was formed the following year, and the swift-skating Swedes went on to capture World Championships in 1953, 1957, 1962, 1967, 1991, and 1992. In the 1994 Olympics, Peter Forsberg, who became a hero with the NHL's Colorado Avalanche in the 1996 Stanley Cup playoffs, defeated the Canadian defender in a sudden-death shootout, giving Sweden its first Olympic gold medal. The Swedes have in fact been at the forefront in many hockey matters. In 1989, for instance, Swede Mats Sundin became the first European chosen first overall in the NHL draft.

Before the Europeans began streaming into the NHL, the league had sent several clubs to Europe on goodwill tours. The Montreal Canadiens and the Detroit Red Wings rode a steamship across the Atlantic in 1938 to play a series of postseason games. The Boston Bruins and the New York Rangers did the same in 1959. The first big influx of European players into the NHL began in the mid-1970s. Swedish defenseman Borje Salming joined the Toronto Maple Leafs in 1973 and proved that European players could keep up in the rough world of the NHL; he became an NHL all-star six times during his career. Other players— Jaromir Jagr from the Czech Republic, Pavel Bure from Russia, Mikael Renberg from Sweden, Jari Kurri from Finland, and Uwe Krupp from Germany—have followed in his footsteps.

In the 1997 draft, teams drafted 19 players from Russia, 16 from the Czech Republic, 15 from Sweden, and 12 from Finland. Slovakia, Ukraine, Germany, Norway, Belarus, Latvia, Switzerland, and Austria combined to have 16 players drafted. Roman Hamrlik of the Czech Republic was drafted by the Tampa Bay . Lightning with their first pick in 1992. Russia's Alexei Yashin and Oleg Tverdovsky were drafted with second picks in 1992 and 1994, respectively.

"Their game and the NHL game are very comparable now," says Bill Barber, who played against the Europeans for Team Canada in the 1976 Canada Cup. "The Europeans have had a chance now to come play in the NHL, and you have to play that style of play if you want to have success. They had more of a puck-control passing game in years past, while we pretty much stayed in our lanes and feasted on turnovers. Plus, we were a little more physical, too."

As a result of the European invasion of the NHL, the games have blended. NHL players have become more freewheeling, and the European players are becoming more physical. That was evident at the 1996 World Cup tournament when Sweden and Russia tried to trade Team Canada punch for punch in their meetings. "The games are becoming so similar because the players have played together so much," says Kurri, who starred for Edmonton, Los Angeles, and Anaheim over the course of his stellar NHL career. "The battles in the corners and the toughness can now be found in Europe, as well as the NHL."

In 1995–96, fans of German players had an especially eventful NHL season. Uwe Krupp of the Colorado Avalanche, the defenseman who scored the winning goal to clinch the 1996 Cup, was the first German-trained player to score a goal in the Stanley Cup finals, and Marco Sturm was the first German-trained player to be selected in the first round of the entry draft. With the marketing and training success that the European clubs had in working with the NHL over the last few years, it wasn't surprising that the IIHF joined the NHL in sponsoring a twelve-country in-line skating tournament in August 1996. (In-line skates are similar to ice skates, but they have wheels in place of blades; they became quite popular in the early 1990s.) Australia, Canada, the Czech Republic, Finland, France, Germany, Italy, Japan, Russia, Sweden, Switzerland, and the United States competed.

In January 1998 the international game went professional for good when the International Olympic Committee permitted pro players to play in the Olympics.

Perhaps the best thing about the worldwide game these days is that players from all countries are learning to play together. "At one point you could tell European players from North Americans by their style of play," says Brian Burke, "They weren't physical. Now those lines have blurred. You look at a player like Vladimir Konstantinov of the Detroit Red Wings. He hits people. I think they've borrowed from our system, and we've borrowed from theirs. They've been a superb addition to the NHL. They've added a level of skill and showmanship, and I don't see that stopping."

Above: Uwe Krupp celebrates after scoring his first Stanley Cup goal.

Opposite: Rugged defenseman Vladimir Konstantinov was a star in the Soviet Union for five years before joining the Detroit Red Wings in 1991. His career ended tragically when he was injured in an auto accident in 1997.

The 1996 World Cup

in a fit of marketing frenzy, the National Hockey League took control of the old Canada Cup tournament, which had been created and developed by player agent Alan Eagleson in the 1970s, and renamed it the World Cup for 1996. The league's goal was to increase hockey awareness around the world, enlarge the fan base in the United States, and promote the game to America's youth. In the fall of 1996, the first World Cup tournament was held, and an amazing thing happened. The United States, long considered a little sister to the Canadians, won the tourney by beating Canada, 2 games to 1, in the championship series. NHL stars packed the roster of practically every team. Brian Leetch, Mike Richter, and John LeClair played for the Americans. Wayne Gretzky, Eric Lindros, and Mark Messier played for the Canadians. Pavel Bure and Sergei Fedorov were on the Russian team, and Peter Forsberg and Ulf Samuelsson were on Team Sweden. Teemu Selanne played for Team Finland. Uwe Krupp played for Germany. Peter Bondra was with Slovakia. And Jaromir Jagr was on the Czech Republic team.

The format was simple. Eight teams were broken into two four-team pools: the North American pool consisted of Canada and the United States, with Russia and Slovakia added to even the alignments; the European pool was made up of the Czech Republic, Finland, Germany and Sweden. After three rounds, the two finalists would meet in a best-of-3 games series. The games were played in Montreal, Philadelphia, Vancouver, New York, Stockholm, Garmisch, Helsinki, and Prague, and the winners received $300,000 Canadian per player.

"It was an amazing success from a lot of different perspectives," says Brian Burke, the director of operations for the NHL. "We got people watching hockey at a time of the year when they historically and traditionally don't. The product was excellent. It displayed the game well and created some new fan interest. The TV ratings were good. From every perspective it was great. Plus, it was some of the best hockey I've ever seen."

The finals between the United States and Canada were a classic battle. The Canadians won Game One in Philadelphia, 4–3, in overtime when Canada's Steve Yzerman beat Mike Richter of the United States at 10:37 of the extra period. Despite an impressive third period by the Canadians—they outshot the Americans, 18–7—the Americans won Game Two, 5–2, at the Molson Center in Montreal. John LeClair scored 2 goals for the United States in that game to increase his tournament totals to 6 goals and 10 points.

The final game, played on September 14, 1996, in Montreal, was called by some observers one of the best non-NHL games ever played. The United States beat the Canadians, 5–2, in one of the most entertaining games ever played. Tony Amonte won the game in the final three minutes by scoring his second goal of the tournament, and Richter, the tourney's most valuable player, stopped an incredible 35 of 37 shots.

The Americans took a 1–0 lead in the first period when Brett Hull beat Canadian goalie Curtis Joseph. Lindros tied the score in the second period with his third goal of the tournament, and Adam Foote put Canada ahead when he scored midway in the third period. But Hull was on fire. The son of Hall of Famer Bobby Hull, Brett tied the score at 2 with just over three minutes to play. Then Amonte netted the game winner. Derian Hatcher and Adam Deadmarsh added insurance goals as the clock ran out.

"I was in awe there," says Rod Brind'Amour, a forward for Team Canada. "That's the kind of thing you dream about when you're a kid. It was excellent to get to know those people on a first-name basis, and it was great to see some of the work ethic that guys like that have. They really work hard, and you can see why they get to the kind of level they're at. A lot of them have that natural ability and are stars. But other guys have to work hard, and that's an impressive thing."

For Bill Guerin, who played winger for the United States, the tournament was an eye-opener. "Just to be involved in something like that is definitely a confidence booster," says Guerin. "Being surrounded by all those great players was definitely a great experience. It was pretty wild just being with those players, but when you're playing against them, you have to see them in a different way. You have to show that you can play hard against them and not hold them in awe. Of course, it's different when you're not on the ice. Those guys—Gretzky, Lemieux, Messier—there is something about them. When they walk into the room and you're with them your confidence just builds up."

Team Canada's Wayne Gretzky takes a hip check along the boards in the 1996 World Cup tournament.

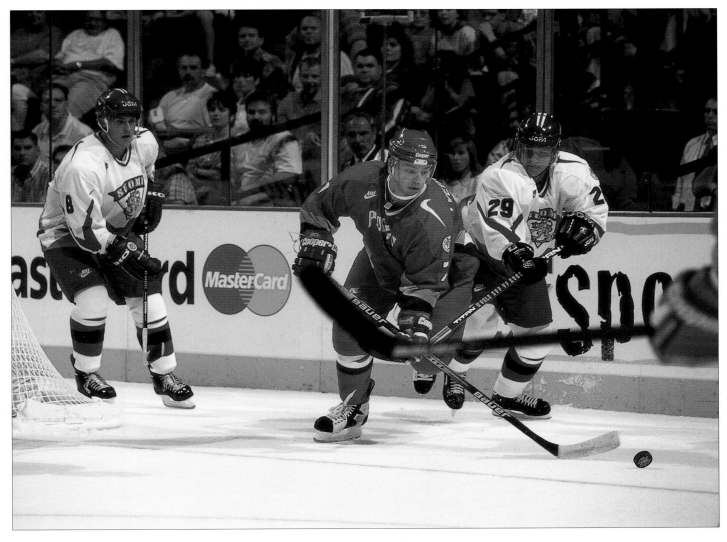

Because the World Cup did not end until their training camps had already started, some players got off to slow starts with their NHL teams. The New York Rangers, who lost a half dozen players to the World Cup, won just 1 of their first 6 games of the 1996–97 season. Lindros injured his groin in the tourney and missed the start of the Flyers' season. Rangers captain Mark Messier said that those tournaments aren't always what they're cracked up to be. "I think that when push came to shove I found it very difficult to play that type of hockey when I knew, two weeks from then, I was going to be back playing with these guys," says Messier. "Don't get me wrong. I wanted to win the World Cup very badly. And I'm not making any excuses for winning and losing. But Brian Leetch and Mike Richter were two of the best players for the United States. So, to go out and take Leetchie's head off, I found that very difficult."

Ron Wilson, coach of the U.S. team, says that people made too much out of the slow starts by many players in the 1996 season. "Did the World Cup really make guys stumble?" Wilson says. "To an extent, yes. But I saw other guys doing well. Joe Sakic, Keith Tkachuk, Derion Hatcher, and Chris Chelios. They all played great at the start of the '96 season."

Scotty Bowman, the winningest coach in NHL history, likes the idea of the World Cup. "I was a little concerned because there are so many European players playing in the NHL," says Bowman. "Initially, it was the intrigue of where these players are from. But I think the emergence of the U.S. team really helped the tournament."

These European players competed in a four-team pool in the 1996 World Cup that included clubs from the Czech Republic, Finland, Germany, and Sweden.

The 1987 Canada Cup

by 1987, it was well established that Canada and the Soviet Union had the two best hockey teams in the world, and the 1987 Canada Cup was the last tournament in which those two teams would meet. When the Soviet Union broke up, so did its national hockey team. This tournament, because of the quantity of stars on both teams, provided some of the best hockey ever played. Wayne Gretzky, Mario Lemieux, Paul Coffey, and Mark Messier were only a few of the stars on that team. As they had in the Summit Series, the Canadians dropped the first game. Alexander Semak scored in overtime to give the Soviets a 6–5 victory. In a dramatic Game Two, the Canadians blew a 3–1 lead and watched as Valery Kamensky scored the tying goal with just 64 seconds left. Lemieux saved the victory, though, with a goal at 10:07 of double overtime. The Canadians got off to a bad start in Game Three, falling behind by 3 goals. They eventually tied the score and then Lemieux and Gretzky teamed up with just 1:24 to play for the winning goal. Taking a pass from Gretzky, Lemieux smacked a wrist shot past Soviet goalie Sergei Mylnikov's glove.

Team Canada's Mark Messier levels a Soviet defenseman and makes his stand in front of the net.

The 1980 Olympics

Until they defeated Canada in the 1996 World Cup, the proudest moment in the history of U.S. Olympic hockey came at the 1980 Olympics at Lake Placid. Facing a Soviet Red Army powerhouse that had already beaten them badly in an Olympic tune-up, the Americans had little hope of victory. But great goaltending by Jim Craig and a clutch goal by Mike Eruzione were two of the reasons why the Americans, picked as also-rans at best, beat the odds.

The two teams opened the tournament in different pools. The Americans, coached by Herb Brooks, went 4–0–1 in their pool. Bill Baker scored a tying goal with just 27 seconds left in the third period to earn the Americans a tie with Sweden in the first game. After that, the U.S. team won 4 consecutive games

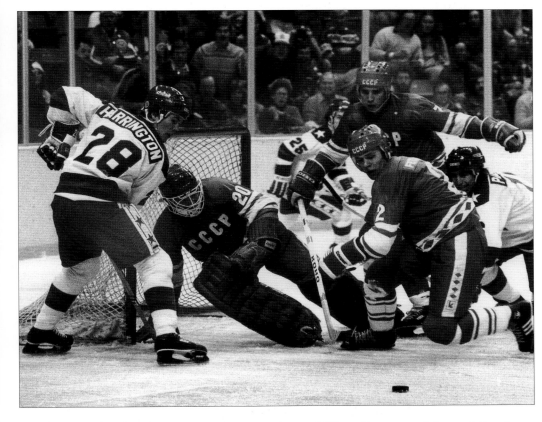

John Harrington of Team USA eyes up a loose puck in front of Soviet goalie Vladislav Tretiak.

against Czechoslovakia, Norway, Romania, and West Germany. Meanwhile, the Russians, who featured the great goaltender Vladislav Tretiak, went 5–0.

The Americans and the Soviets finally met in the semifinals. The Red Army took a 1–0 lead, but the Americans tied it on a goal by Buzz Schneider. The Soviets went ahead, 2–1, but Mark Johnson knocked in a rebound to tie the score at 2. In a move that no one expected, Soviet coach Viktor Tikhonov replaced Tretiak with Vladimir Myshkin in the second period, and the Soviets took a 3–2 lead. Then the Americans got serious. Craig played like a powerhouse in the third period, and Johnson tied the score with his second goal of the game. Eruzione then etched his name in the history books when he took a pass from Mark Pavelich at the top of the circle and scored for a 4–3 victory.

The Americans went on to beat Finland in the gold-medal game, 4–2, and complete the miracle.

The International Game

The 1972 Summit Series

although the Russians had dominated the amateur hockey world by winning games in the Olympics and in the world championships, most of the hockey world believed that Canada in 1972 was the home of the world's best players. It was Canada that stocked the NHL with nearly all of its stars, and its extensive network of junior and minor-league teams provided the perfect training ground for young players. But the Russians, organized by their military, had also developed an effective training system, and they agreed to play the Canadians in an 8-game challenge to be called the Summit Series. The first 4 games would be played in Montreal, Toronto, Winnipeg, and Vancouver. The second 4 would be played in Moscow. The winner could claim to be the world's best team.

The Canadians, even without the injured Bobby Orr, were confident. But their confidence flagged a bit in Game One at Montreal when their 2–0 lead turned into a 7–3 victory for the Russians. Canada, with Harry Sinden serving as general manager, won Game Two in Toronto, 4–1, to even the series. The Russians bounced back to tie Game Three in Winnipeg and then, to the amazement of North America, win Games Four and Five. The Canadians were in trouble until defenseman Paul Henderson, never known as a scorer, came up with two dramatic game-winning goals in Games Six and Seven in Moscow. The Russians, facing final defeat, took an early lead in Game Eight. Phil Esposito and Yvon Cournoyer scored for the Canadians to tie the game. Then Henderson scored his third straight game winner and earned a place in Canadian history.

Canada finally won the tournament, 4–3–1, but the Russians had won the respect of the hockey world.

Below: Forwards Frank Mahovlich (27) and Phil Esposito of Canada watch the bouncing puck in front of the Soviet goal. Esposito scored in the final game of the dramatic eight-game series to help the Canadians beat the Soviet Union.

Opposite: The United States Olympic team celebrates after upsetting the Soviet Union in a semifinal game on February 22, 1980. The Americans would go on to win the gold medal.

Pros in the Olympics

With the inclusion of professional players in the Olympics in the 1998 Games in Nagano, Japan, the best players were on show for the entire world to see. Gone were the rags-to-riches story of the 1980 U.S. team that won the gold medal. Gone were the hopes of a young boy to play college hockey and represent his country in the world's greatest athletic event. But it seems that Olympic organizers think the fans want to see professional players. "People want to see the best," says coach Scotty Bowman. "Let's face it. For years the Olympic athletes weren't really amateurs. They were as pro as the next guy."

Brian Burke of the NHL sees the Olympics as a great vehicle to attract new fans. "The focus that the Olympics draw is amazing," says Burke. "Take gymnastics. I don't like gymnastics, but I watched the U.S. gymnasts. What the Olympics will do is offer the same quality of hockey as the World Cup but for a much larger audience. It will be a great shot of adrenalin for the sport worldwide."

Ron Wilson agrees with Bowman and Burke. "It's great exposure," Wilson says. "It was not a fair tournament because the Russians always had their pros, call them what they want. The deck was always stacked against the United States and Canada and some of the other countries. From a fairness point of view, since everybody has a different definition of professionalism and amateurism, this is

The bench for Team Canada watches the action in the 1994 Olympics in Lillehammer, Norway. The Canadians settled for a silver medal after losing to Sweden in the championship game's sudden-death shootout.

the best way." Wilson understands the allure of the Olympics to young players. "I liked having twenty-year-old guys on the team and that was like a stepping stone to the next level," Wilson says. "You viewed it as a goal to play in the Olympics, and you didn't have to be one of the twenty best players in your country at that age. Now, you've got to be one of the twenty best. Period. That really limits kids realizing their dreams and playing in the Olympics." So now Wilson urges young players to look past the Olympics to a professional career.

Says Jari Kurri, "It's a great idea for the fans. They get to see the best players in the world." Pat Conacher disagrees, saying that pro players in the Olympics takes away some of the tournament's romance. For years, Conacher worked out in Calgary at a Canadian Olympic training site. He met hockey players, figure skaters, and skiers and was impressed by their work ethic and love of the sport. He doesn't like to see NHL players take away their chances for rare athletic glory. "People don't realize how disciplined and focused those athletes have to be," Conacher says. "I think the pros should stay out of it. I know it's all money. I like the idea of the pros. They should still go play in the pro leagues. But stay there. Athletes in the pro leagues are making good money. Why not give an amateur athlete a chance to experience an Olympic dream? Let those people, who train hard and don't get paid, have their days in the sun. A lot of kids won't go on to play pro hockey, but they still have Olympic dreams."

In Nagano, the American pros got off to a rough start. They disgraced themselves by trashing their rooms and causing $3,000 worth of damage after being eliminated in the quarterfinals by the Czech Republic, the eventual gold medal winners. After that, the Olympic organizers had second thoughts about inviting the pros to play again. Canada lost the bronze medal game in 1998 to Finland, and Russia settled for the silver medal.

Slovakia's Zigmund Palffy is flipped upside down after being sandwiched between Sweden's Daniel Ryamark (left) and teammate Robert Svehla during an Olympic game on February 13, 1994.

The NEW WAVE

"I think the next wave of superstars is secure."

BRIAN BURKE,
director of hockey operations for the NHL

One of the most endearing aspects of sports is its regenerative nature. When the players we grew up watching finish their careers, other athletes, young and strong and eager to follow in the footsteps of our older heroes, take their places. This is not a sad event. We know that time catches up with all of us, and that athletes are ravaged by time and circumstance sooner than most of us. So we celebrate their passing from the game and the addition of their replacements.

The "replacements" in the National Hockey League have made the game even faster and more exciting than it was before. "The game is pretty safe in the hands of these players," says Terry Murray. "There are still some real quality veterans in the league, but they're getting older. The group that is there coming up, with Eric Lindros and Peter Forsberg and Jaromir Jagr and the younger guys, we know the game is in good hands. The game is just getting better. The speed of the game, the size and strength of the players, their overall conditioning—all of it is much better. The game is growing throughout the world and moving forward very quickly. Going into the next century, the game of hockey is moving up."

Eric Lindros

After being drafted first overall by the Quebec Nordiques in the 1991 draft, the 6-foot-4 (1.9m), 236-pound (107kg) center sat out the 1991–92 season after refusing to play for Quebec. At the 1992 draft, the Nordiques traded Eric Lindros to the Philadelphia Flyers in the biggest deal in NHL history—six players, two number one picks, and $15 million went to Quebec in the transaction—and the center racked up 41 goals as a rookie for the Flyers. A punishing checker, Lindros suffered knee injuries early in his career and played in no more than 73 games in each of his first four seasons. But he scored more than 40 goals in three of the seasons and, in the lockout season of 1994–95, with 29 goals in 46 games, won the Hart Trophy as the league's most valuable player.

Because the Flyers lacked depth in Lindros's first few seasons, the young center showed only flashes of being a franchise player, one that could carry a team on his back to the finals. Indeed, the "Legion of Doom" line, which consisted of Lindros, left winger John LeClair, and right winger Mikael Renberg, dominated the NHL for two seasons. But the Flyers could get no farther than the Eastern Conference finals in Lindros's first four seasons. In the last of those four seasons, he scored 115 points.

In 1997, Lindros led the Flyers to the Stanley Cup finals only to lose in four straight games to the Detroit Red Wings. Despite the disappointment, he said he learned a valuable lesson. "You go through a game and do your best and try to learn from it," Lindros says. "Every game you learn something. It's like having 82 classes of school each year. It's good for teams to find their identity together.

Eric Lindros has the rare combination of power, speed, grace, and skill.

They appreciate it when they get there. A lot of teams laughed at us when we got outplayed, got smoked. But we knew it was going to change, and when it did, it felt a whole lot better."

Jaromir Jagr

The 6-foot-2 (1.9m), 216-pound (98kg) Jaromir Jagr was born in Kladno in the Czech Republic, but soon after his move to the United States, he won the hearts of every hockey fan in Pittsburgh. Drafted fifth overall by the Penguins in the deep 1990 draft, Jagr teamed with Mario Lemieux and the rest of the offense-minded Penguins to win Stanley Cups in 1991 and 1992. The 1995–96 season was a breakthrough year for the right winger. He exploded for 62 goals and 87 assists as he and Lemieux amazed the NHL. The flamboyant Jagr, with his long, curly hair flowing from beneath his helmet, became an instant hit with the Penguins fans. He would hang out with them in bars and restaurants after the games, drinking with them and sharing his love of fast cars. Jagr showed his goal-scoring touch as soon as he entered the league. He had 27 goals as a rookie and didn't drop below 32 for the next six seasons. Jagr showed true sportsmanship in 1995 when, accepting the Art Ross Trophy for most points in the season, he said that Lindros should have at least shared in accepting the award. Both players had 70 points, but Jagr won the trophy by scoring more goals, 32–29.

Now that Mario Lemieux has retired, the Penguins need Jaromir Jagr to do even more.

Few goal scorers are as tough in the trenches as Keith Tkachuk.

Keith Tkachuk

A rough-and-ready left winger who can score and fight with the best in both departments, Keith Tkachuk was the foundation of the Winnipeg Jets before they became the Phoenix Coyotes in 1996. Now that they're the Coyotes, Tkachuk will be the foundation of that team. The 6-foot-2 (1.9m), 210-pounder (95.3kg) was drafted nineteenth overall by the Jets in the 1990 draft, and he turned out to be an instant hit. He has soft hands and is great at controlling the puck. He racked up 28 goals in his first full season—he spent much of 1992 playing for the U.S. Olympic team—then notched 41 and 50 goals in two of his next three seasons. Perhaps even more impressive are his penalty-minute numbers. Tkachuk, who won most of the fights he got into, had more than 200 penalty minutes in three of his first five seasons and more than 150 in the other two. Throughout all his physical play, Tkachuk has been an iron man, playing in 372 games in his first five full NHL seasons.

Paul Kariya

Paul Kariya was the number one draft pick of the Mighty Ducks of Anaheim and the fourth overall pick of the 1993 draft. It took exactly one season for this 5-foot-11 (1.8m), 175-pound (79.4kg) left winger to dominate his team, and just two seasons to dominate in the NHL. After scoring 18 goals in 47 games in the lockout season of 1994–95, Kariya poured in 50 goals and added 58 assists in 1995–96. He was a first-team All-Star in 1996 and 1997, and he won the Lady Byng Trophy as the league's most gentlemanly player with a high level of production in 1996 and 1997. He was the only NHL rookie to lead his team in scoring in 1995, and he led all rookies in goals. Unlike the physical Tkachuk, Kariya plays a finesse game. In 1996–97, he had just 6 penalty minutes in 69 games. What Kariya does best is skate and pass. He's one of the fastest skaters in the league, and teammates are often caught unaware when one of Kariya's nifty passes appears from out of nowhere. Here's more bad news for opposing defensemen: Kariya patterns his style of play after Wayne Gretzky.

Smooth as silk, Paul Kariya turns skating into an art.

Ed Jovanovski

A big, physical defenseman who took on Lindros—and won—in the 1996 play-offs, Ed Jovanovski was the first pick overall in the 1994 draft when he was chosen by the expansion Florida Panthers. After returning to his junior hockey team for one more year of seasoning, Jovanovski joined the Panthers just in time for their 1996 run to the Stanley Cup finals. The 6-foot-2 (1.9m) 205-pounder (93kg) scored 10 goals and had 11 assists in 70 regular-season games that year. He added 8 assists in the playoffs, but his greatest asset was his physical play and puck-handling ability. Jovanovski doesn't like to just hit opposing players, he likes to punish them. He skates well and uses his feet skillfully to control pucks that get lost in his skates.

Ed Jovanovski, a first-team all-star in the Ontario Hockey League in 1995, was named to the NHL's 1996 all-rookie team.

Jim Carey

At 6 feet 2 inches (1.9m), 205 pounds (93kg), Jim Carey is big for a goaltender, and he came up big for the Washington Capitals in 1995–96. Carey went 35–24–9 that season, just his second in the NHL, and picked up a league-high 9 shutouts. He added a 2.26 goals-against average and won the Vezina Trophy as the league's best goaltender. Selected by the Capitals in the second round of the 1992 draft—he was thirty-second overall—Carey went 18–6–3 as a rookie and had a 2.13 goals-against average. Carey is best known for his great glove hand.

Chris Osgood

Chris Osgood dueled with Jim Carey for the top goaltending honors during the 1995–96 season and lost narrowly in most departments. But he had a fine season for the Detroit Red Wings. He went an amazing 39–6–5, with a 2.17 goals-against average and 5 shutouts. Rotating for several seasons with teammate Mike Vernon, Osgood rolled up fine statistics in his first three years. After being drafted fifty-fourth overall in the 1991 draft, the 5-foot-10 (1.8m), 160-pound (72.6kg) Osgood was 23–8–5 in 1993–94. He went 14–5 the next season and dropped his goals-against average down to 2.26. Osgood finished with a record of 23-13-9 in 1996-97, but Vernon was named the most valuable player of the 1997 Stanley Cup finals.

Above: While defensemen Paul Coffey and Nicklas Lidstrom watch, Chris Osgood makes the save on a shot by Wendel Clark.

Opposite: Jim Carey was traded from Washington to Boston in March 1997 in one of the biggest deals of the 1996-97 season. Here he makes a stop while still with the Capitals.

Chris Pronger

At 6 feet 5 inches (2.0m), 220 pounds (100kg), Chris Pronger is one of the biggest defensemen in the NHL, and many hockey people expect him to develop into one of the best. He had 11 goals and 24 assists for St. Louis in 1996–97, but his best trait is banging into forwards and knocking them off balance. Pronger is a fine skater and smart enough not to make the turnover mistakes that plague many young defensemen. Pronger was Hartford's first pick and the second over- all in the 1993 draft. The Whalers tired after just two seasons of waiting for Pronger to blossom, but all indications are that he can become a franchise player.

Peter Forsberg

Peter Forsberg scored 10 goals in the 1996 playoffs to help the Colorado Avalanche win the Stanley Cup in 4 games against the Florida Panthers. Part of the deal that sent Eric Lindros from Quebec to the Flyers, Forsberg became an instant star as soon as he joined the NHL. Actually, Forsberg was a star even before he joined the league with the Quebec Nordiques. After dominating the Swedish League for three seasons, Forsberg was called the greatest player *not* in the NHL. Once he joined the league, he had no trouble fitting in. He had 30 goals and 86 assists in 1995-96 and 28 goals and 58 assists in 1996-97. The 6-foot (1.8m), 190-pounder (86.2kg) was the Flyers' first pick and the sixth overall in the 1991 draft, but he skates and protects the puck like a seasoned veteran. He sees the ice well, isn't afraid to mix it up in the corners, and has amazing poise for a player his age.

Above: Chris Pronger looks for a safe pass.

Opposite: Peter Forsberg, one of the most complete players in hockey, sets up between New Jersey goaltender Martin Brodeur and center Neal Broton.

Martin Brodeur

The first-round pick of the New Jersey Devils and the twentieth overall in the 1990 draft, Martin Brodeur won the Calder Trophy in 1994 as the NHL's top rookie by going 27–11–8 and racking up a goals-against average of 2.40. When the Devils won the Stanley Cup in 1995, Brodeur went 16–4 in the postseason and averaged just 1.67 goals per game. The 6-foot-1 (1.8m), 205-pounder (93kg) had three shutouts in the 1995 playoffs and went 37-14-13 in 1996-97 regular season. One of Brodeur's secrets in making big stops is to stand up straight in the net and provide the shooter with a big target to hit. He uses his stick well to control the puck around the net and usually keeps a cool head under fire.

Martin Brodeur led the NHL with 10 shutouts in 1996-97. He is also one of four goalies in NHL history to score a goal.

What Does the Future Hold?

Brian Burke, the director of hockey operations and vice president of the NHL, will be one of the men who will keep tabs on these superstars of the future, and he's certain that the game is in good hands. "People who watched hockey twenty or thirty years ago will argue that many of our players aren't as creative with the puck as players were then," says Burke. "I don't know if that is true or not, but I can tell you one thing: the average player today is faster, bigger, a better skater, and shoots harder. In every single area that you can measure physical ability, the

athletes today are far superior. And that won't change. When I'm at the draft and these kids come up on the stage, I'm 6-foot-2 [1.9m] and I'm looking up at a lot of them. I'm looking at all the first- and second-round defensemen and I'm saying, 'Holy Cow. What did their moms feed these kids?' I think the next wave of superstars is secure, and that's important. You have to pass the torch. As one generation of stars goes out, it's important that there be another wave ready to grab that torch. With these younger players we have that group."

Who knows? Perhaps one of these kids playing between periods of an NHL game will be the player to take the game to the next level.

Bibliography

The American Hockey League. *The 1995–96 American Hockey League Official Guide and Record Book.* Endwell, NY: Carr Printing, 1995.

Associated Features, Inc. *Inside Sports Hockey.* Detroit: Visible Ink Press, 1997.

Diamond, Dan and Peter McGoey. *Hockey: The Illustrated History.* Toronto: Doubleday Canada Limited, 1985.

Diamond, Dan. *The Official National Hockey League Stanley Cup Centennial Book.* Buffalo, NY: Firefly Books, 1992.

Fischler, Stan and Shirley Fischler. *Everybody's Hockey Book.* New York: Charles Scribner's Sons, 1983.

Jacobs, Jeff. *Hockey Legends.* New York: Michael Freidman Publishing Group, 1995.

The National Hockey League. *National Hockey League Official Rules 1995–96.* Chicago: Triumph Books, 1995.

The National Hockey League. *The National Hockey League Official Guide and Record Book 1995–96.* Chicago: Triumph Books, 1995.

The World Cup of Hockey. *World Cup of Hockey Media Guide 1996.* Scarborough, Ontario: Moore Data Management Services, 1996.

Photography Credits

Index

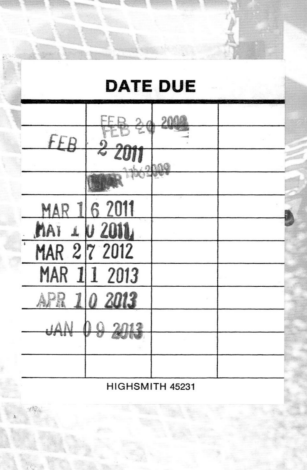